Progressive

Complete

Learn to Play

Harmonica

Manual

By
Peter Gelling

Visit our Website
www.learntoplaymusic.com

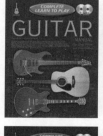      

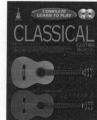      

The Progressive Series of Music Instruction Books, CDs, and DVDs

PROGRESSIVE COMPLETE LEARN TO PLAY HARMONICA
I.S.B.N. 1 86469 238 3
Order Code: CP-69238

Acknowledgments
Photographs: Phil Martin

For more information on this series contact;
L.T.P. Publishing Pty Ltd
email: info@learntoplaymusic.com
or visit our website;
www.learntoplaymusic.com

CONTENTS

CONTENTS CONTINUED

CONTENTS CONTINUED

CONTENTS CONTINUED

For more books and recordings by Peter Gelling, visit: **www.bentnotes.com**

INTRODUCTION

Progressive **COMPLETE LEARN TO PLAY HARMONICA** is the ultimate harmonica manual. It assumes you have no prior knowledge of music, and will take you **from beginner to professional level**. In the course of the book you will learn **all the essential techniques of diatonic and chromatic harmonica playing** along with how to read music, how to improvise and how to analyze music and musical forms. By the end of the book you will be ready to play in a band, understand improvisation and be competent in a variety of musical styles.

The book is divided into sections, the first covering basic rhythms, techniques, and reading, and an introduction to forms such as the 12 bar Blues. The later sections cover expressive techniques, improvisation and explanations of chords, scales and keys. Each new technique is introduced separately and all examples sound great and are fun to play. The examples and solos demonstrate a variety of styles including Blues, Jazz, Rock, Country, Folk and Classical. The accompanying CD's contain all the examples in the book so you can play along with them. The book also features a chart listing all fingerings for the saxophone. **All harmonica players should know all of the information contained in this book.**

The best and fastest way to learn is to use this book in conjunction with:
1. Buying sheet music and song books of your favourite recording artists and learning to play their songs. By learning songs, you will begin to build a repertoire and always have something to play in jam sessions.
2. Practicing and playing with other musicians. You will be surprised how good a basic drums/bass/guitar/harmonica or simply harmonica and guitar combination can sound even when playing easy music.
3. Learning by listening to your favourite CD's. Start building a collection of albums of players you admire or wish to emulate. Try playing along with one of them for a short time each day. Most of the great harmonica players have learned a lot of their music this way.

Also in the early stages it is helpful to have the guidance of an experienced teacher. This will also help you keep to a schedule and obtain weekly goals. To help you develop a good sense of time it is recommended that you **always** practice with a metronome or drum machine.

USING THE COMPACT DISCS

This book comes with **two compact discs** which contain all the examples in this book. The book shows you which holes on the harmonica to play and what technique to use and the recording lets you hear how each example should sound. Practice the examples slowly at first, gradually increasing tempo. Once you are confident you can play the example evenly without losing the beat, try playing along with the recording. You will hear a drum beat at the beginning of each example, to lead you into the example and to help you keep time. A small diagram of a compact disc with a number as shown below indicates a recorded example. Some of the tracks on the CD contain more than one example. In these cases, index points have been used (1.0, 1.1, 1.2 etc). If your CD player has an index points function, you can select each example individually. If not, each example will automatically follow the previous one.

23.0 ← CD Track Number

APPROACH TO PRACTICE

Regardless of the style of music you play, it is important to have a correct approach to practice. You will benefit more from several short practices (e.g. 20-30 minutes per day) than one or two long sessions per week. This is especially so in the early stages, because of the basic nature of the material being studied and also because your lips and facial muscles are still developing. If you want to become a great player you will obviously have to practice more as time goes on, but it is still better to work on new things a bit at a time. Get one small piece of information and learn it well before going on to the next topic. Make sure each new thing you learn is thoroughly worked into your playing. This way you won't forget it, and you can build on everything you learn.

In a practice session you should divide your time evenly between the study of new material and the revision of past work. It is a common mistake for semi-advanced students to practice only the pieces they can already play well. Although this is more enjoyable, it is not a very satisfactory method of practice. You should also try to correct mistakes and experiment with new ideas. It is the author's belief that the guidance of an experienced teacher will be an invaluable aid in your progress. To develop a good time feel, it is essential that you always practice with a metronome or a drum machine.

TYPES OF HARMONICAS

There are several different types of harmonicas and each one has its own unique sound. In this book you will learn how to play the **diatonic ten hole harmonica,** and the **chromatic harmonica**. Both are shown in the photos below. Diatonic harmonicas are the most common and are best for note bending and Blues playing as well as Country and Folk music. They are tuned in one specific key, although it is possible to play in at least four different keys on one diatonic harmonica. The first three sections of the book deal with diatonic harmonica playing using a **C harmonica**.

The final section of the book deals with chromatic harmonica playing. Chromatic harmonicas are often associated with more complex styles such as Jazz, but are also used in Soul, R&B and Pop (e.g. Stevie Wonder). The chromatic harmonica is not usually associated with note bending. In fact, bending notes on a chromatic harmonica can damage the instrument. It is possible to play in all keys on the chromatic harmonica by using the **slide**, which is depressed (pushed in) to create extra notes

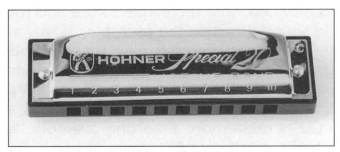

Diatonic Ten Hole Harmonica

Chromatic Harmonica

SECTION 1
Basic Techniques, Rhythms and Sounds

THE DIATONIC HARMONICA (KEY OF C)

The first three sections of the book will teach you how to play a **diatonic ten hole harmonica,** which is the most common type of harmonica. It is also the best type for bending notes and several other techniques essential for harmonica playing. There are many different brands of diatonic harmonica available. Some of my personal favorites are the **Hohner marine band** or **special 20** models, and the **Lee Oskar** by **Tombo.** The body of the instrument may be made of either wood or plastic. Although some players prefer the wooden body, the plastic version is more practical because it can be washed without any swelling of the body. When the wood swells, the edges of each block can become rough and can cut your mouth. With plastic, this does not happen. The CD which accompanies this book has been recorded with a **C harmonica.** This means that a harmonica with a **C** written on it (as shown below) is tuned to the key of C. The word "key" means the central note to which all others relate. There are twelve different keys used in music and each one begins on a different pitch. To play along with the CD you will need a C harmonica, so make sure your harmonica has a C written somewhere on it.

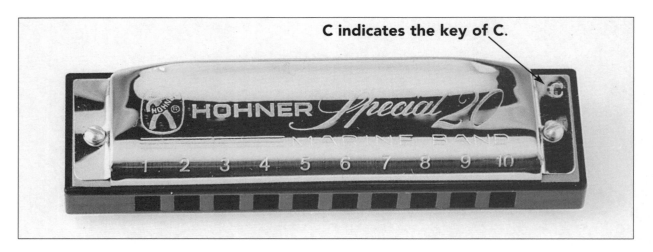

C indicates the key of C.

HOW TO HOLD THE HARMONICA

The best way to hold the harmonica is shown below, using the **left hand**, with the low numbered end of the harmonica held gently between your thumb and forefinger. The numbers on the harmonica should be facing upward. This hand position will prepare you to use the sound effect known as the **hand vibrato** or **wah wah**, which is introduced in lesson 4. It can be used by right or left-handed players alike. Keep the four fingers of the left hand straight, and pressed gently but closely together, with no visible gaps between them.

LESSON ONE

MAKING MUSICAL SOUNDS

The harmonica is capable of producing both **notes and chords**. A **note** is the sound produced by inhaling or exhaling on any one hole of the harmonica. A **chord** is a combination of three or more notes played together. In some situations it is desirable to play **two** notes together. This is called a **double stop**. Each of these possibilities requires a different technique to produce the correct sound. These different methods will be dealt with as the book progresses. The easiest thing to play on the harmonica to begin with is a chord. To locate a particular three hole chord, simply place your mouth at the centre note of the chord, allowing your mouth to cover a comfortable amount of the harmonica. For example, to play a chord using the **4**, **5**, and **6** holes, centre your mouth on the number **5** hole. The number **4** and **6** holes will automatically be included. If you are unsure what holes you are covering, try placing your tongue in one of the holes, then replace it with your finger and have a look to see which hole it is. After doing this a few times you will soon become familiar with which holes you are sounding.

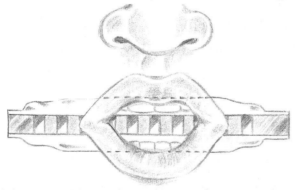

1.0   Low, Middle and High Chords

The first example on the accompanying recording is a demonstration of chords played with exhale and inhale breaths in the low, middle and high sections of the harmonica. To imitate what you hear on the CD, start with an inhaled note on holes **1**, **2** and **3**, followed by exhaled notes and then move up the harmonica, then back down. Don't worry at this stage about exactly what holes you are playing, just get a feeling for where you should move to produce higher or lower sounds. This first example is not notated, listen to the CD and copy the sounds you hear. As you play, make sure the harmonica points directly into your mouth as shown below rather than being angled. This will allow the air to flow freely through the instrument as you breathe and will produce the clearest sound.

READING THE NOTATION SYSTEM

This book uses a unique harmonica notation system which gives you specific information about which holes to play to get the correct sounds and how long to hold each note for. The system is made up of a combination of numbers corresponding to the holes on the harmonica, and rhythm notation which is closely related to standard musical notation.

The holes on the harmonica are represented by **two types of numbers**.

Outlined numbers indicate notes played with an **inhaled breath**, e.g. ② indicates the second hole on the harmonica inhaled.

Solid numbers indicate notes played with an **exhaled breath**, e.g. **2** indicates the second hole on the harmonica exhaled.

Chords are indicated by numbers stacked vertically one on top of the other, e.g. ③②① indicates that holes 1, 2 and 3 are played **simultaneously** with an inhale breath.

The length of time a note or chord should sound is indicated by standard musical notes placed under the hole numbers, as shown below.

5 Hole 5 exhaled   ⑥ Hole 6 inhaled

    Held for value of **Half note**   Held for value of **Quarter note**

Any **added expression markings** (slides, bends, trills, etc) are placed above the hole numbers in italics, e.g. a bend on hole 4 inhaled would be notated as shown below.

Here is a list of all the expression markings used in the book. Each one of these techniques is introduced individually in the course of the book in the appropriate lesson.

V   Indicates **hand vibrato**

S   Indicates **slide**

B   Indicates **half step bend**

B̄   Indicates **whole step bend**

T   Indicates **trail off**

Tr   Indicates **trill**

W   Indicates **grace note** (mouth wah bend)

BAR LINES

Bar lines are drawn vertically across the notation, which divides the music into sections called **bars** or **measures**. A **double bar line** signifies either the end of the music, or the end of an important section of it.

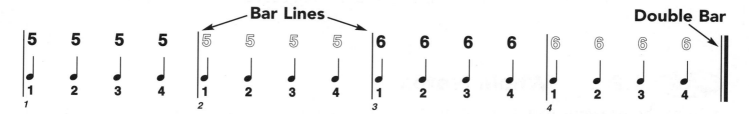

THE FOUR FOUR TIME SIGNATURE

These two numbers are called the **four four time signature.** They are placed at the beginning of standard music notation. The 4/4 time signature tells you there are four beats in each bar. There are **four** quarter notes in one bar of music in 4/4 time.

THE QUARTER NOTE

Count: 1

This music note is called a **quarter note**. It lasts for **one** beat. There are four quarter notes in one bar of 4/4 time.

This example contains chords played in quarter notes exhaling and inhaling on holes 1, 2 and 3. As you play the example, all of your air should be directed through your mouth and harmonica, with none escaping through your nose, or around the corners of your mouth. Tap your foot and count mentally as you play to help make sure that all the notes are of equal length. The two dots just before the double bar at the end of this example are called a repeat sign and indicate that the example is to be played again from the beginning.

 1.1

Repeat Sign

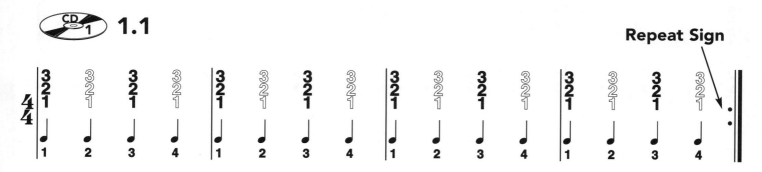

THE WHOLE NOTE

o

Count: **1** 2 3 4

This is a **whole note**. It lasts for **four** beats.
There is **one** whole note in one bar of $\frac{4}{4}$ time.
The whole note is the longest note commonly used in music.

 1.2   **Whole Notes**

As with the previous example, count mentally and tap your foot as you play to help you keep time. Make a habit of this with each new thing you learn.

THE HALF NOTE

This music note is called a **half note**. It has a value of **two** beats.
There are **two** half notes in one bar of $\frac{4}{4}$ time.

Count: **1** 2

Be sure to hold the whole note in the last bar of this example for its full value. It should end where you would count **1** for the next bar if there was a following bar. This principle can be applied to all notes which last for one beat or more: i.e. the note ends right on the count of the following note or rest.

 1.3   **Half Notes**

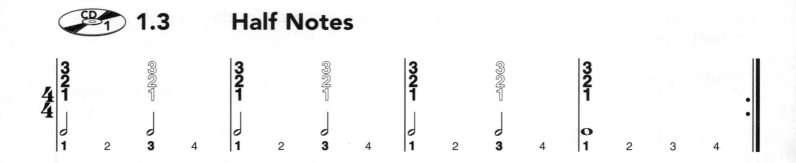

CONSECUTIVE BREATHS

Many times in harmonica playing you will find situations where you play chords or notes which require the use of consecutive inhale or exhale breaths. Because we naturally breathe in, out and in again, this can be difficult at first. In the following example, chords are played in quarter, half and whole notes with consecutive exhale breaths and consecutive inhale breaths.

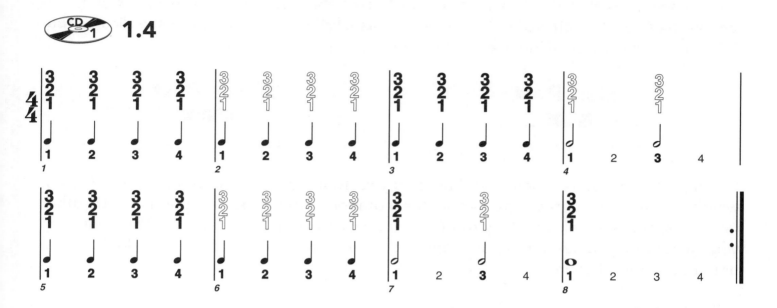

This example contains a combination of consecutive and alternate **i** and **e** breaths. Take it slowly at first if necessary. Tap your foot as you play and make sure your beat remains steady regardless of whether you are playing inhale or exhale notes. The more you do this, the easier it becomes.

LESSON TWO

RESTS

Rests are used to indicate silence in music. There are different rests for different lengths of silence just as notes indicate different lengths of sound. The symbols below are very similar. The difference is that the **half rest** sits **on top of the line**, while the **whole rest** hangs **below the line**. The **half rest** indicates **two beats of silence**. The **whole rest** indicates **four beats or a whole bar of silence**. Small counting numbers are placed under rests.

It is important to keep counting and tapping your foot steadily on each beat regardless of whether a note or a rest appears in the notation. When you are playing with other musicians, someone else is likely to be playing while your part has a rest. When you play your next note, you need to be perfectly in time with them. This is difficult to do if you are not in the habit of counting.

2.0 Whole and Half Rests

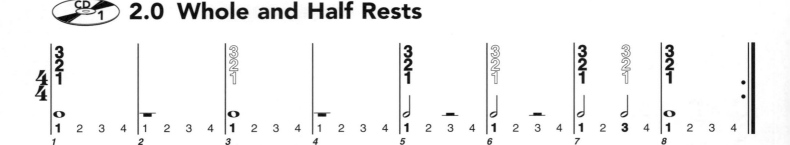

MOVING BETWEEN POSITIONS

So far, everything you have played has been on the lowest three holes of the harmonica. The following example moves between this position and a position one hole further up where your mouth is covering holes **2**, **3** and **4**. Another important thing to notice here is that rests give you a natural place to take a breath if you need it. Try to get into the habit of breathing where rests occur, rather than in between written notes.

2.1

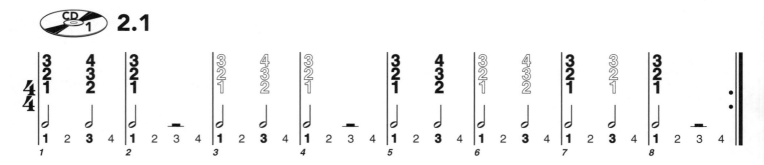

PLAYING SONGS

Here is the first part of the popular children's song **Three Blind Mice**. Playing this song requires several changes of mouth position. Once again, take it slowly at first and breathe where rests occur.

3 **Three Blind Mice**

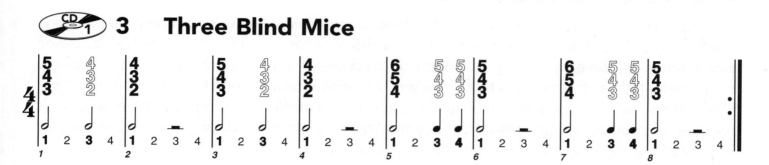

THE QUARTER REST

Count: 1

This symbol is a **quarter rest.** It indicates **one beat of silence**. Do not play any note. Remember that small counting numbers are placed under rests.

The following song makes use of the quarter rest. Once again the rest provides an opportunity to breath without disrupting the flow of the music. Because the quarter rest lasts for only one beat, you will need to be quicker with your breath to make sure you play the next note or chord in time.

Be sure to count and tap your foot as you play. This will help you keep time regardless of whether notes or rests occur in the notation.

4 **Mary Had a Little Lamb**

LESSON THREE

PLAYING SINGLE NOTES

Playing single notes is often difficult at first. Most people will still have a second note sounding the first time they attempt single notes. In time the muscles around your lips will develop and single notes will be easy to play, but don't be surprised if you have trouble at first. To play a single note, tighten the muscles that circle your mouth to form a round hole as pictured below. The mouth position used is similar to that used for whistling. Although some tension is required to produce single notes, your eventual goal should be to have all muscles as relaxed as possible, using only the minimum pressure necessary.

The easiest hole to begin playing single notes on is number **1** at the low end of the harmonica. This is because you only have to block the unwanted extra notes on one side of the hole.

 5.0

This example demonstrates the difference between single notes on hole **1** and chords.

 **5.1**

Here, only single notes are used. These are the notes produced by exhaling and inhaling on hole **1**. The names of these notes are C and D. Since there are no rests in this example, the best place to take a breath is at the end of each whole note. This is common when playing melodies.

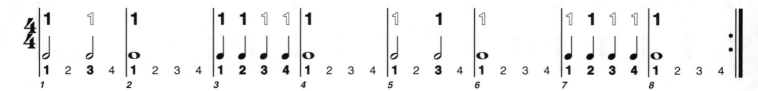

5.2

Once you are confident with the previous example, try this one which moves between holes **4** and **3**. Because these notes have other notes either side of them this may be more difficult, so be patient and keep practicing and you will soon have it under control.

6 Three Blind Mice - Version 2

Here is the first part of **Three Blind Mice** played in single notes. Don't worry if you are finding it difficult to produce single notes clearly without extra notes sounding at this stage. This is very common. It takes time for your lips and facial muscles to develop, so practice often but for short periods. Soon you will have single notes well under control and you will be able to play many melodies.

7 Ode to Joy

This popular melody is the main theme to Beethoven's ninth Symphony.

THE THREE FOUR TIME SIGNATURE

3/4 This time signature is called the **three four** time signature. It tells you there are **three** beats in each bar. Three four time is also known as waltz time. There are **three** quarter notes in one bar of 3/4 time.

THE DOTTED HALF NOTE

A **dot** written after a note extends its value by **half**.
A dot after a half note means that you hold it for **three** beats.
One dotted half note makes one bar of music in 3/4 time.

Count: 1 2 3

The following song **Beautiful Brown Eyes** is a typical example of the way dotted half notes are used in 3/4 time. As there are no rests in the first three lines of this example, you could breathe at the end of any of the dotted half notes if you need to. Listen as you play each song and try to find the most natural sounding places to breathe. The final bar of this song contains a whole rest. In 3/4 time, a whole rest indicates a whole bar rest.

CD 1 8 Beautiful Brown Eyes

Here is another song in ¾ time. This one has a sad kind of tonality known as a **minor key**. This term will be dealt with in lesson 20. Don't be too concerned with the terminology for now, just be aware that each different kind of sound has a name in music. If you are curious, ask a musical friend or music teacher about each of the terms you encounter here.

9 Minor Mood

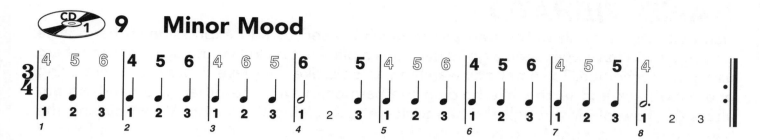

THE LEAD-IN

Sometimes a song does not begin on the first beat of a bar. Any notes which come before the first full bar are called **lead-in notes** (or pick-up notes). When lead-in notes are used, the last bar is also incomplete. The notes in the lead-in and the notes in the last bar add up to one full bar. The following song is an early Jazz standard made popular by brass bands in New Orleans. It contains **three lead-in notes**. On the recording there are **five** drumbeats to introduce this song.

10 When the Saints go Marchin' in

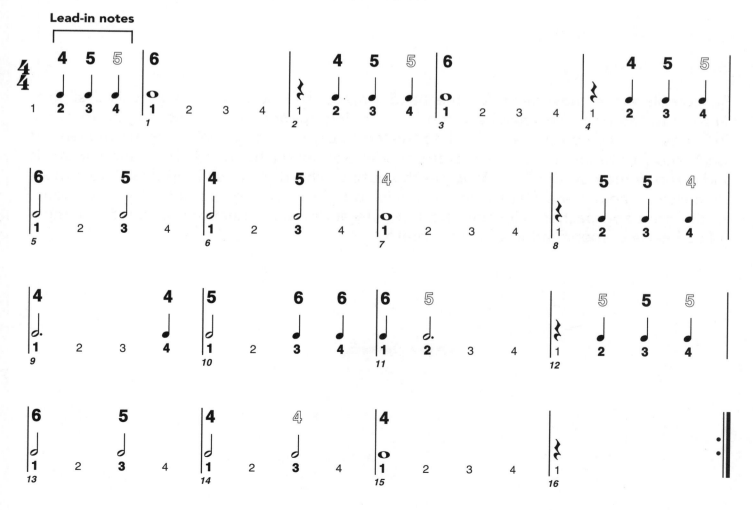

LESSON FOUR

HAND VIBRATO

Hand vibrato or "wah wah" is an effect which is used to add expression to harmonica playing. If you have ever seen a good harmonica player, it is likely that you have seen them using this technique. To somebody watching, it looks like the player is waving or fluttering one hand back and forth while holding the harmonica with the other. The hand vibrato alters the flow of air through the harmonica, thus altering the sound. When playing the hand vibrato, the right hand is moving between two basic positions. The first is formed by cupping the right hand around the left in its normal holding position, as shown in the diagram below. The heels of both hands should be touching and the right hand fingers should curl up along the left hand little finger and around and upwards past the end of the left hand little finger and ring finger. This position results in the air being closed off by the two hands.

To complete the movement for the hand vibrato, the right wrist is swivelled slightly around to the right. This results in the "cup" being opened up and allowing air through. The wrist can then be swivelled back to the left to close the cup again. It is this movement back and forth that causes the vibrato or wah wah effect to sound. The hand vibrato is indicated in the notation by a **V** above the note or chord to which it applies. Experiment with slow, medium and fast vibrato, there is no right or wrong speed for this technique, as different approaches will sound best in different musical situations. Listen to example 14 to hear a demonstration of hand vibrato.

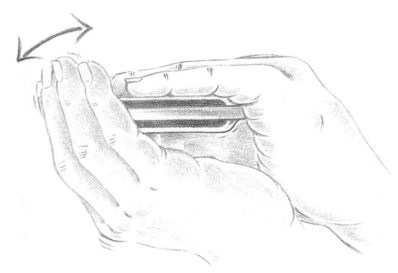

11.0 **Hand Vibrato**

This example uses the hand vibrato on both notes and chords. Listen to the recording to hear the difference between notes played without vibrato and notes played with vibrato.

The most common place the hand vibrato is used is on sustained notes such as whole notes, as demonstrated in the following song.

11.1 **Banks of the Ohio**

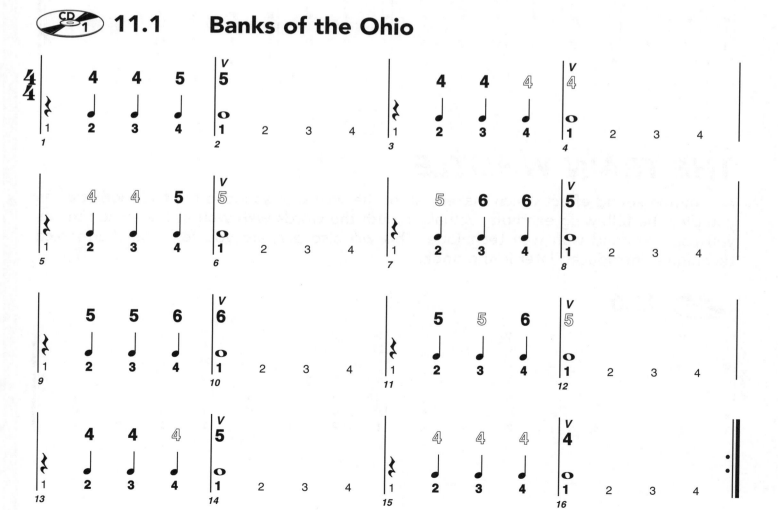

Here is another song to practice your hand vibrato with. This one is in 3/4 time and has no vibrato markings above the notes, so it is up to you where you use it. The best place is wherever a half note occurs (e.g. bars 5 and 8) as quarter notes do not really give enough time for the vibrato to be heard. Try adding hand vibrato to other songs you know.

11.2 Streets of Laredo

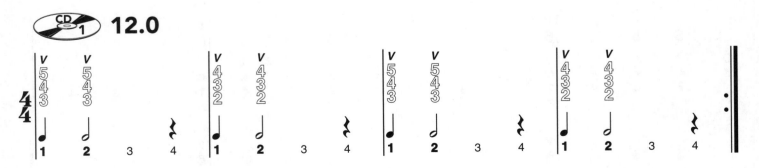

THE TRAIN WHISTLE

A common sound effect which makes use of the wah wah sound is the **train whistle**. As you play the following example, actually mouth the words **wah wah** at the same time as you use the hand wah wah technique. This will also prepare you for other harmonica techniques introduced later in the book.

12.0

THE TIE

The following example demonstrates the use of **ties**. A **tie** is a curved line which connects two different notes of the same pitch. The tie tells you to play the **first** note only, and to hold it for the length of both notes. A tie may occur either **across a bar line**, or **within one bar**. The use of ties is the only way of indicating that a note or chord is to be held across a bar line. Don't forget to count as you play so you know how long you have held each note for.

12.1

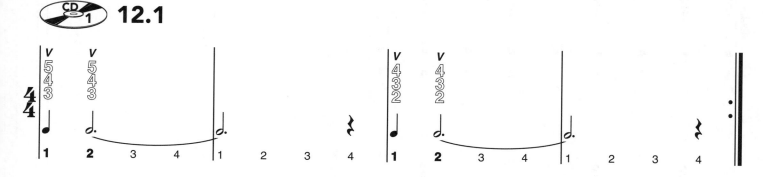

12.2

This example combines the train whistle with a simple train rhythm. The harmonica is a great instrument for imitating the sounds of the steam train. There is a whole tradition of this style of playing and if you can do it, you will be sure to have everybody's feet moving!

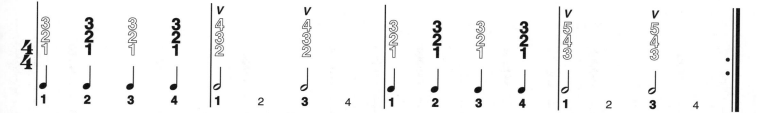

COMBINING CHORDS AND SINGLE NOTES

The next step in developing the train rhythm is to combine chords and single notes, specifically the hole 1 **inhale** note. There are also many other musical situations where you will need to alternate between chords and single notes, so take your time and learn this example carefully.

12.3

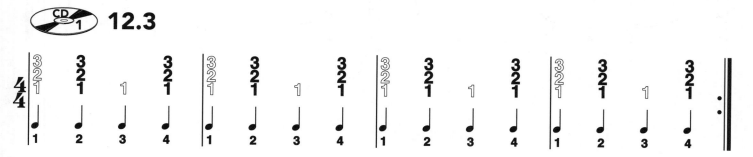

26

Now try this solo which makes use of all the train sounds you have learnt. Take it slowly at first and then build up speed as you become more confident.

13 I Hear the Train a Comin'

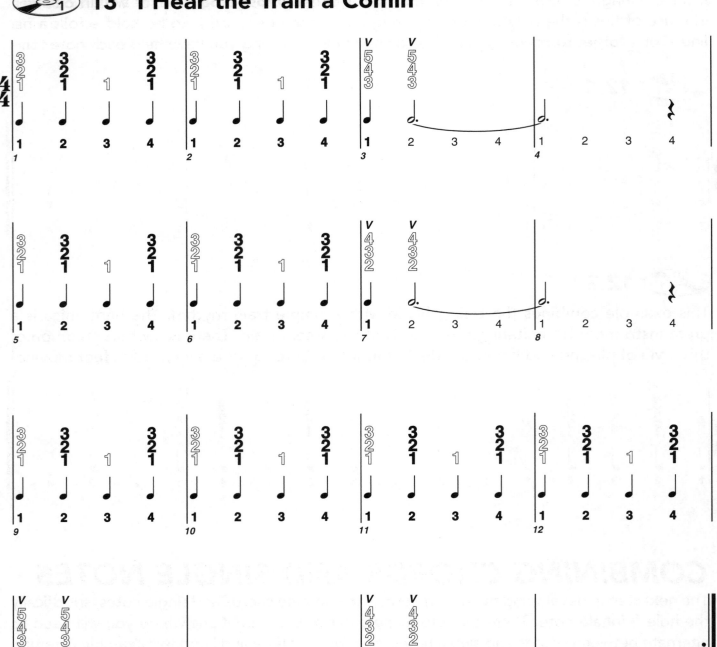

TONGUING

Everything you have played up to this point has been done by simply inhaling or exhaling through the harmonica. However, there are several other techniques used to produce notes on the harmonica. The most important of these is **tonguing**. This means articulating the sound of each note with the tongue by saying **ta** as you play. Listen to the following example on the CD to hear the difference between notes and chords played without the tongue and then with the tongue.

CD 1 14.0

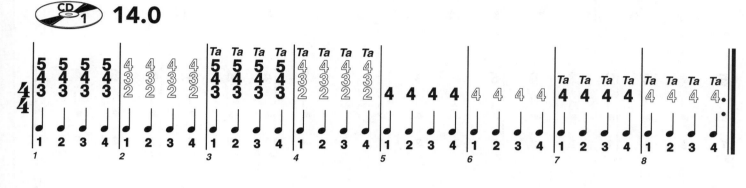

CD 1 14.1

Here is a single note exercise to help you become more confident with the tonguing technique. Remember to say **ta ta ta ta** to get the correct sound when tonguing.

It is important to be able to play a melody equally well whether you are tonguing the notes or not. Practice the following melodies both ways. Make sure all your notes sound clear and even in volume and time.

15.0 Cockles and Mussels

15.1 Will The Circle Be Unbroken

This song contains many tied notes which provide good opportunities to use hand vibrato.

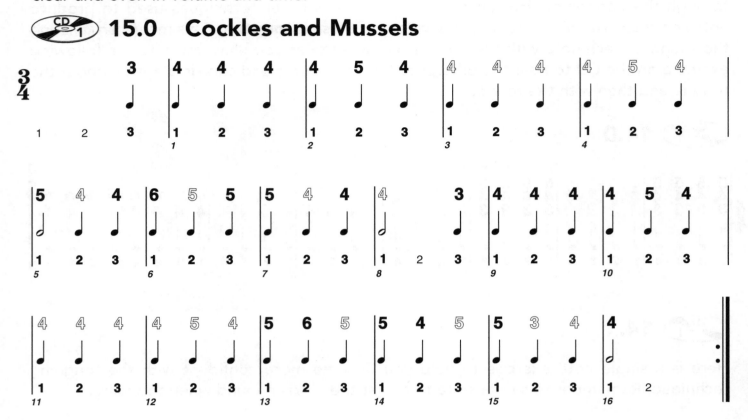

SECTION 2
More Complex Rhythms, Scales, Blues Playing

LESSON FIVE

THE EIGHTH NOTE

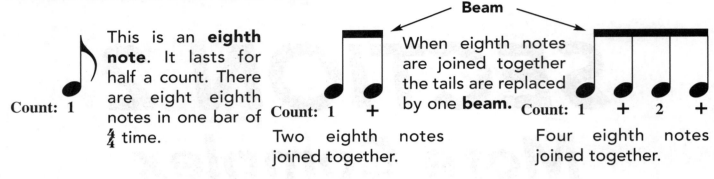

16 How to Count Eighth Notes

Here is a song using eighth notes in 3/4 time. Remember to count mentally and tap your foot as you play. Take it slowly at first.

17 Lavender's Blue

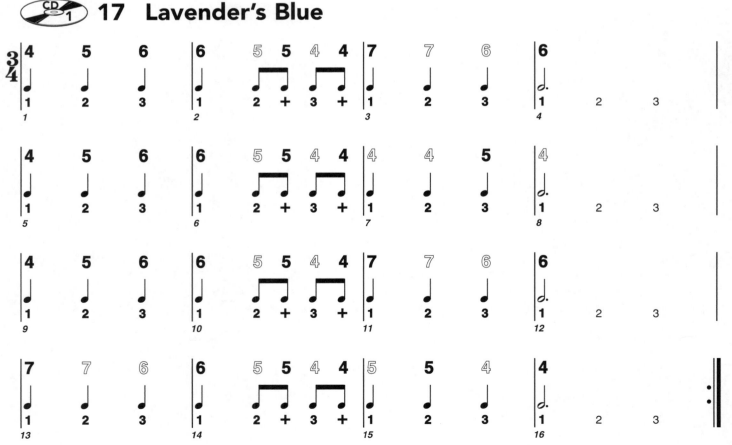

Here are two more pieces featuring eighth notes. Take them slowly until you can play each one correctly and then gradually increase the speed until you can play along with the recording.

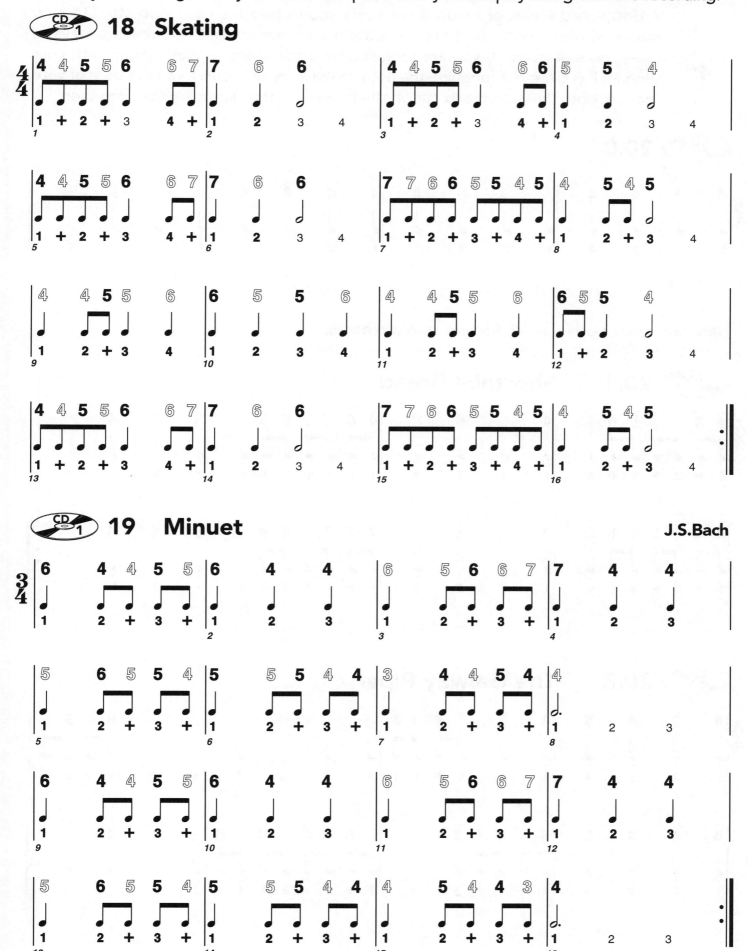

18 Skating

19 Minuet

J.S.Bach

STACCATO

A dot placed above or below a note tells you to play the note **staccato.** Staccato means to play a note short and separate from other notes. There are two ways to play a note staccato. If you are tonguing the note, make a "**dot**" sound with your tongue. If you are not tonguing the note, make a "**huck**" sound with the back of your tongue. Both these methods cut off the flow of air, thus stopping the note short.

20.0

Here are two melodies which feature staccato notes.

20.1   **Shortnin' Bread**

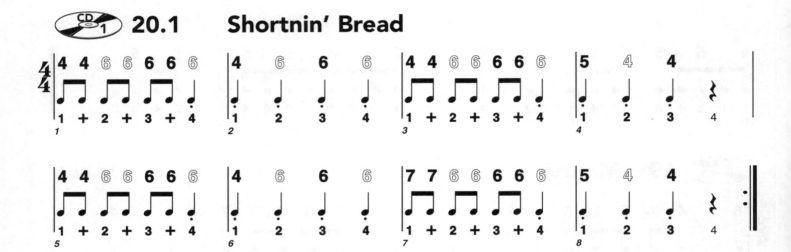

20.2   **The Galway Piper**

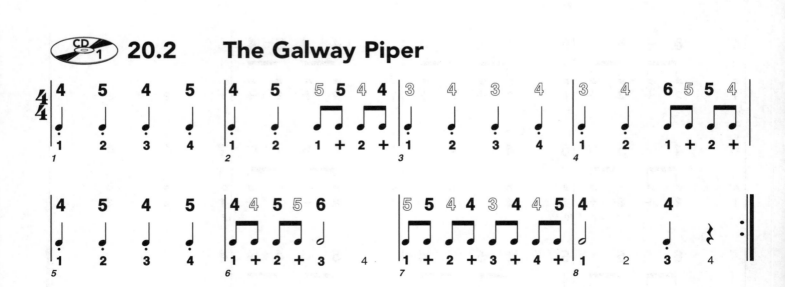

DOUBLE TONGUING

Another useful technique for articulating notes is called double tonguing. This technique is used by many wind instrument players and is just as valuable on the harmonica as it is on the trumpet or saxophone, **especially when playing train rhythms**. Double tonguing means playing each group of two notes with a "ta ka" sound. The first note is articulated with the front of the tongue (**ta**) and the second note is articulated with the back of the tongue. Try saying **taka taka taka taka** several times before playing the following example.

21.0

21.1

Here is a variation containing ties which is also useful for playing train rhythms. Take it slowly at first.

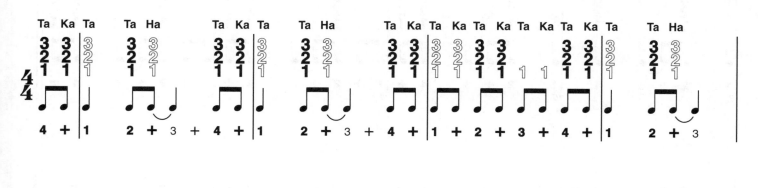

etc.

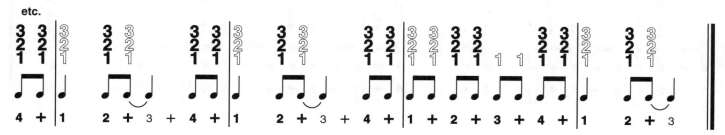

34

Here is a train rhythm solo complete with whistles, making use of the techniques you have just learnt. Practice the rhythms slowly with a metronome and tap your foot on each beat to help you keep time. Once you have it under control, increase the tempo until you can play it along with the recording. There are many possible variations on these rhythms, so practice making up your own as well.

22 Freight Train Stomp

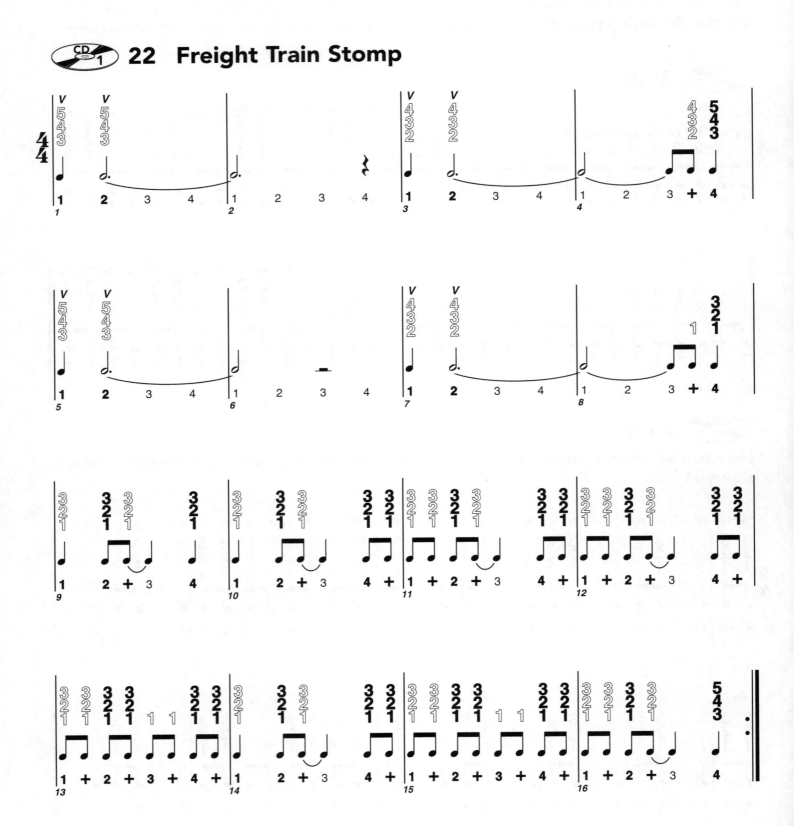

LESSON SIX

12 BAR BLUES

12 Bar Blues is a pattern of chords which repeats every 12 bars. There are hundreds of well known songs based on this chord progression, i.e., they contain basically the same chords in the same order. 12 bar Blues is one of the most common progressions in Blues, Jazz and Rock. Every harmonica player will be regularly asked to play a 12 bar Blues. In fact it is very likely to be the first kind of song used at any jam session. The following example demonstrates a common 12 bar Blues riff played on the harmonica. A **riff** is a pattern of notes which repeats and may be altered slightly to fit the chords.

CD 1 **23.0** **12 Bar Blues**

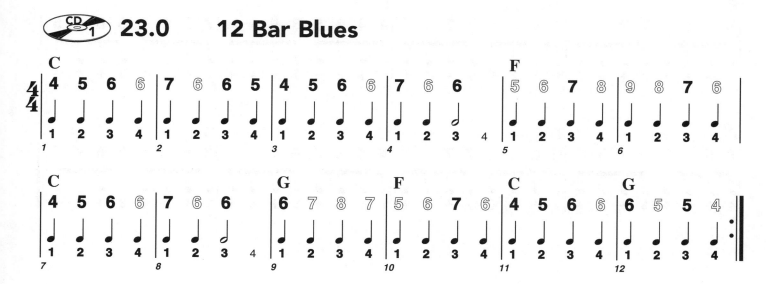

One of the classic sounds in Blues music is the combination of harmonica and guitar. When you play any riff or melody on a 12 bar Blues progression, your notes are fitting in with a specific set of chords which can be played by a guitar (or keyboard). The chords most commonly played by the guitar are built on the first, fourth and fifth notes of the key you are playing in. These chords are often described by the use of roman numerals. If you are playing in the key of C, these chords will be C (Ⅰ), F (Ⅳ) and G (Ⅴ). A detailed explanation of notes and chords as scale degrees is given in lessons 11 and 12. The easiest way to start recognising the relationship between notes and chords is to remember that each time you begin playing a riff on a C note (hole **1**, **4** or **7** exhale), the guitar will most likely be playing a **C chord**, which is simply the C note with two additional notes on top of it. When the note and chord are played together, a harmonious sound is produced. In the following examples, chord symbols for the chords C, F and G are written above the notation to show which chords a guitar would play to accompany the harmonica. The basic pattern of the 12 bar Blues is shown below.

Ⅰ	Ⅰ	Ⅰ	Ⅰ
Ⅳ	Ⅳ	Ⅰ	Ⅰ
Ⅴ	Ⅳ	Ⅰ	Ⅴ

Here is a variation on the previous 12 bar Blues riff, this time using eighth notes. Since there are no longer notes in this example, you will need to take a quick breath at the end of every second bar.

 23.1   **12 Bar Blues Using Eighth Notes**

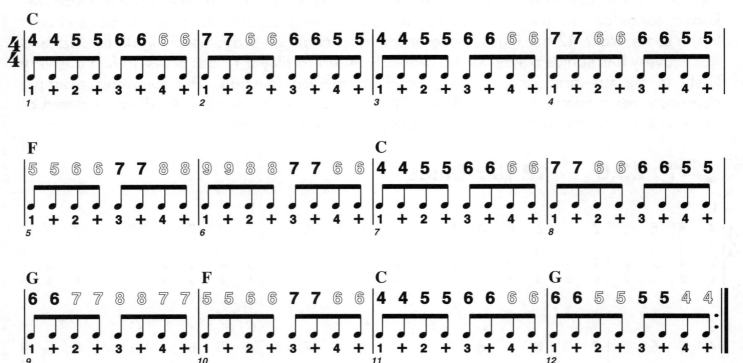

THE EIGHTH REST

   This is an **eighth rest**.
It indicates **half a beat of silence**.

 24.0

All the chords in this example are played on the **and** (**+**) part of the count.

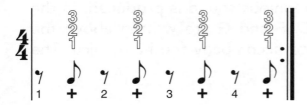

 **24.1**

This 12 bar Blues makes use of both quarter and eighth rests. The only notes in this example are **C**, **F** and **G**, which are the notes on which the chords for a 12 bar Blues in the key of C are built.

 **25.**

Here is another Blues using eighth rests. This one is a rhythm part which works well with a guitar or a whole band.

RHYTHM PLAYING

Here is another Blues rhythm part, this time using half, quarter and eighth rests. This type of playing is very effective when another musician is playing a solo. The use of longer rests leaves space for other instruments to be heard. This is an important principle in music generally. If everyone played constantly, the music would sound chaotic and claustrophobic. Learning where to play and where to leave space takes time and experience. Listen to how the musicians interact on your favorite albums and practice what you hear when you are playing with others.

CD 1 **26.**

BREATH CONTROL

One of the most important elements of harmonica playing is a consistent and relaxed approach to breathing and breath control. A good player always produces a strong, even tone and sounds relaxed regardless of the difficulty of the music being played. Outlined below are some breathing exercises which will help you gain more control over the way you breathe when playing and give you a solid consistent approach which will eventually become automatic, enabling you to forget about breathing and concentrate totally on the music you are making.

A good way of developing your breathing technique is the use of visualisation. When you breathe **in**, think of an inflatable life raft which fills automatically when you pull out the plug. This will help you equate breathing in with relaxation. When you breathe **out**, think of a tube of toothpaste being slowly squeezed from the end (not the middle). This will help you use your breath economically in a controlled manner.

It is important to develop the habit of controlling your breathing from your diaphragm muscle (shown in the diagram below). As you breathe **in**, let the diaphragm relax downwards and allow the lungs to fill with air right to the bottom. Then breathe **out slowly**, squeezing gently from the diaphragm (like the tube of toothpaste) and see how long you can sustain your outgoing breath. The more control you have of your diaphragm, the easier you will find breathing when you play.

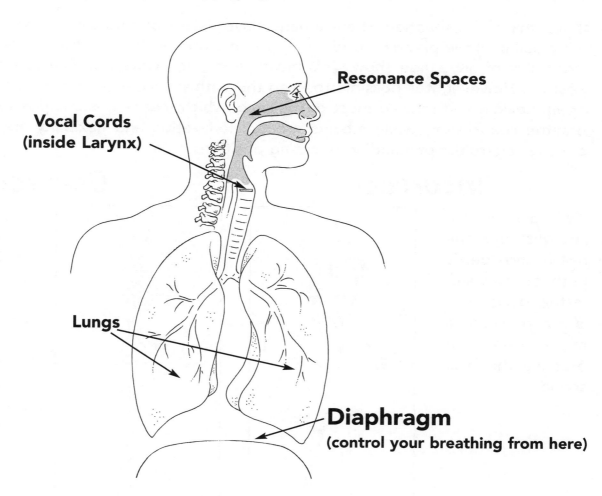

Resonance Spaces

**Vocal Cords
(inside Larynx)**

Lungs

Diaphragm
(control your breathing from here)

OTHER USEFUL EXERCISES

When playing wind instruments, it is common to use more air, movement and muscle activity than necessary. There are two common exercises which are useful for learning to use less force and less air when playing. The first of these is to slowly blow up a balloon, using slow sustained breaths controlled from the diaphragm. The idea is to take a comfortable breath using the technique described earlier and then breathe into the balloon using an even sustained amount of air pressure. Repeat this until the balloon is full.

The second exercise is to **sing** a melody in front of a lighted candle. This requires a more subtle release of air than blowing up a balloon, as the idea is to sing with as little effect on the flame of the candle as possible. Once you can sustain a note without moving the flame much, try beginning the note softly and gradually increasing the volume, then reverse the process. You could also try singing a whole verse from a song. As with all aspects of musicianship, be patient and you will see great improvement as long as you continue to practice.

POSTURE

The term "posture" refers to the way the body is held (e.g. straight, slumped, etc) and its position when sitting or standing. For playing wind instruments, it is best to stand rather than sit, as this allows the most open and unrestricted passage of air for both breathing and sustaining notes. If you are playing guitar or keyboards along with your harmonica, you may have to sit. In this situation, it is essential to sit up straight but relaxed, as this will produce the best sound.

If you think of a situation where a harp player is performing with a band, it would look fairly dull if all the players stood straight in the one position all the time. Movement is a large part of any stage show. This means it is not always possible to maintain perfect posture. However, it is possible to keep the pathway from the diaphragm to the mouth open, flexible and relaxed most of the time, which means it is still possible to play and breathe comfortably while moving around. Relaxation and flexibility are keys to good posture regardless of standing or sitting position.

Incorrect   Correct

The spine is not straight and the head and pelvis both tilt forward. In this position, it is not possible to move freely or produce the best sound.

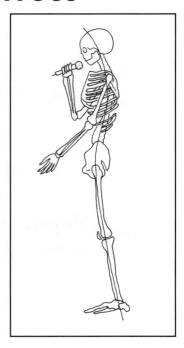

The spine is comfortably straight and in line with the head, legs and pelvis. This position keeps the airways open and makes movement easy and comfortable.

LESSON SEVEN

THE C MAJOR SCALE

The **Major Scale** is a series of eight notes in alphabetical order that has the familiar sound:

DO   RE   MI   FA   SO   LA   TI   DO

The notes of the major scale are easy to find on the harmonica. You have already played many tunes derived from the C major scale. The following example demonstrates the sound of the C major both ascending and descending. It is worth memorising the pattern of holes used to produce the major scale. This helps to identify how to play sounds by ear, which is an important part of harmonica playing. The scale starts on hole **4** and continues up to **7**. It mostly consists of an exhale breath followed by an inhale breath, except for the notes La (6) and Ti (7) which are both inhale breaths. When you reach the higher Do (7) you have played **one octave** of the major scale. An octave is the range of 8 notes of the major scale. The lower and higher Do are said to be one octave apart.

27 C Major Scale

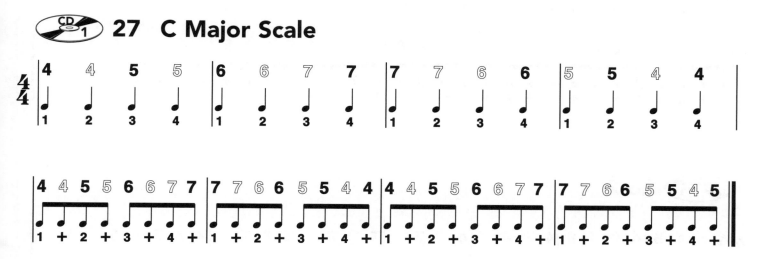

The C major scale consists of the following notes.

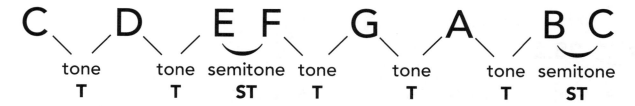

The distances between the notes are measured in tones (or whole steps) and semitones (or half steps). These are the basic building blocks for scales in all keys. As the terms would suggest, a tone or whole step is made up of two semitones or half steps. An understanding of whole and half steps becomes more important when it comes to note bending (discussed in lesson 11) as these are the two possible distances notes are usually bent on the harmonica.

There are literally thousands of melodies which can be played using only the notes of the C major scale. It is extremely important to know all of the notes of this scale well and to be able to change between the notes easily. The following examples are designed to help you develop this skill.

28.0

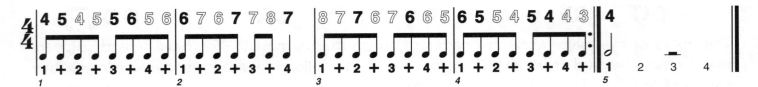

28.1

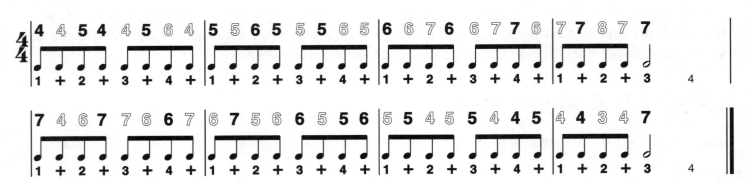

28.2

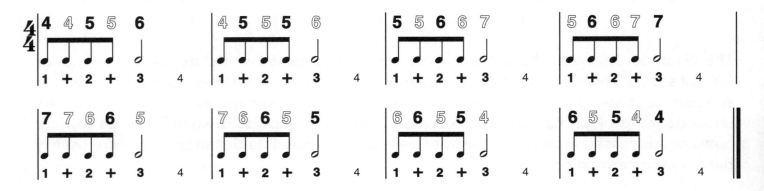

28.2

 29 **Botany Bay**

The notes of this traditional Australian song all come from the C major scale. If you listen to the recording, you will hear the guitar playing chords as an accompaniment. These chords are all built on notes from the C major scale also.

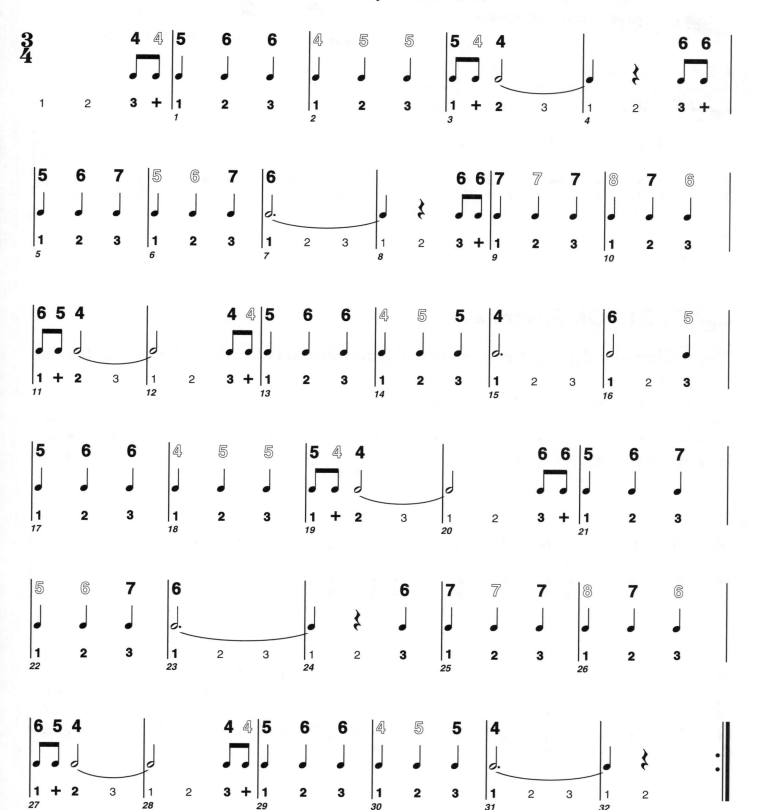

THE DOTTED QUARTER NOTE

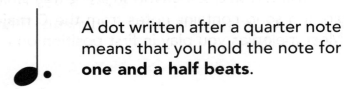

A dot written after a quarter note means that you hold the note for **one and a half beats**.

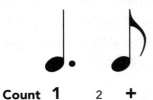

A dotted quarter note is often followed by an eighth note.

Count 1   2   +

30.

31 Oh Susanna

This well known folk song makes use of the dotted quarter note followed by an eighth note.

KEY OF C MAJOR

When a song consists of notes from a particular scale, it is said to be written in the **key** which has the same name as that scale. For example, if a song contains notes from the **C major scale**, it is said to be in the **key of C major**. Most melodies you play in first position on a C harmonica will be in the key of C major.

CD 1 32   **Morning Has Broken**

SYNCOPATION

The following example demonstrates a different use of the dotted quarter note. This time an eighth note is followed by the dotted quarter. This creates an effect known as **syncopation** which means displacing the normal flow of accents from on the beat to off the beat. Syncopated rhythms can be difficult at first, so count and tap your foot as you play.

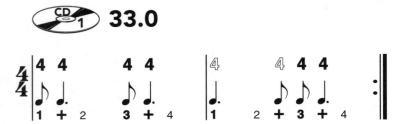

33.0

33.1   Swing Low, Sweet Chariot

This song makes use of both of the dotted quarter note figures presented in this lesson. It is played at the very top end of the harmonica. Take it slowly at first and count as you play.

Another common method of creating syncopated rhythms is to use ties as shown here.

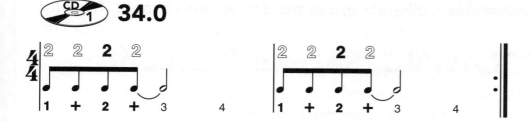

34.0

34.1 Jamaica Farewell

This well known Caribbean song contains many syncopated rhythms created by the use of both rests and ties. If you have trouble with syncopated rhythms, play them on one note first and count as you play.

LESSON EIGHT

CROSS HARP PLAYING (Second Position)

On any harmonica, it is possible to play in more than one key even though there is a specific key written on the harmonica. This is because there are a variety of different sounds used in music and the major scale is only one of these sounds. The most common way of playing in another key is to use what is called **second position** or **cross harp**. This method is essential for Blues playing and is also used for other styles such as Country and Rock. When you play cross harp on the C harmonica, C is no longer the key note. The note G now becomes the key note. The note G can be found at holes 2, **3**, **6** and **9** (see lesson 15 for detailed description). This method of playing can take some time to get used to, but is essential if you wish to pursue techniques such as note bending. The train imitation sounds you have already played have been cross harp in the key of G, so you're halfway there already! If you are playing a 12 bar Blues in the key of G, the guitar would be playing the chords G (Ī), C (ĪV) and D (V̄). On page 120 there is a chart showing which key harmonica to choose for cross harp playing with every key used in music. The following 12 bar Blues in the key of G uses the cross harp position to play a riff based around the notes G, C and D which are the **root** (foundation) notes of the chords played by the guitar to accompany the harmonica.

35.0   12 Bar Blues in G

Here is a 12 bar Blues in the key of G which contains whole notes along with quarter notes and quarter rests. It makes use of notes on holes 1, 2, 3 and 4.

MORE ABOUT 12 BAR BLUES

As you learned in lesson 6, the **12 bar Blues** is a pattern of chords which repeats every 12 bars. A **chord** is a group of three or more notes played together. It is possible to play chords on the harmonica and also many other instruments including the guitar and keyboard instruments such as organ and piano. Usually an accompaniment to any melody or solo contains chords (e.g. guitar accompaniment to harmonica melody). The chords in that accompaniment come from the same key as the melody and are often built from the major scale of that key.

When you play cross harp, you are playing in the key of **G**. This means that all the scale degrees for cross harp playing relate to the note G. This means that the chords for the accompaniment will come from the G Major scale which is shown below.

G Major Scale

G	A	B	C	D	E	F♯	G
1	2	3	4	5	6	7	8

CHORD NUMBERS

When you play any riff or melody on a 12 bar Blues progression, your notes are fitting in with a specific set of chords which can be played by a guitar (or keyboard). The chords most commonly played in Blues are built on the **first**, **fourth** and **fifth** notes of the key you are playing in. These chords are often described by the use of roman numerals. If you are playing in the key of **G**, these chords will be **G** (Ⅰ), **C** (Ⅳ) and **D** (Ⅴ).

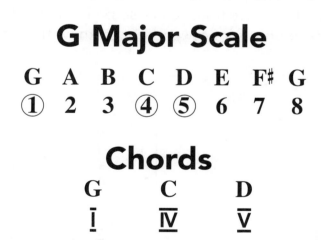

G Major Scale

G A B C D E F♯ G
① 2 3 ④ ⑤ 6 7 8

Chords

G	C	D
Ⅰ	Ⅳ	Ⅴ

Sometimes you may see other types of chord symbols such as **G7** (seventh chord) or **G9** (ninth chord). These are other types of chords which are common in Blues. The number in the chord symbol describes the type of chord but does not affect the position of the chord in the key. For example, any chord starting with the letter **G** will be chord Ⅰ in the key of G regardless of whether the chord is G, G7 or G9.

Understanding this system of numbering chords is particularly useful for learning how to play melodies which follow the 12 bar Blues structure and sound good with any accompaniment. The diagram below shows the typical positions of chords Ī, IV̄ and V̄ within the 12 bar form. The IV̄ chord in the second bar is optional. When this chord is used, it is often called a "Quick IV̄". It is a good idea to memorize the progression shown below, so you will always know what chord you are playing over. When you think you know the progression well, give yourself a quiz, e.g. what chord is in bar six? (IV̄), bar nine? (V̄), bar three? (Ī), etc.

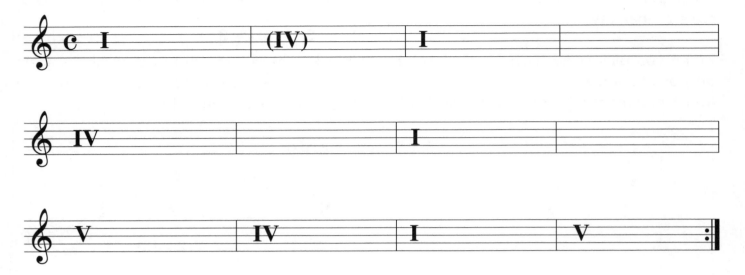

ROOT NOTES

The note a chord is named from is called the **root note** (like the root of a tree). A good way to memorize a chord progression is to play only the root notes of the chords all the way through the progression. An example of this is shown below. Since chords Ī, IV̄ and V̄ in the key of G are G, C and D, you will first need to locate these notes on your harmonica. To begin with, G (Ī) can be found on holes 2 and 3, C (IV̄) can be found on holes 1 and 4, and D (V̄) can be found on holes 1 and 4. These notes can also be found in other places higher up on the harmonica, but stick to these ones for now and get to know them thoroughly.

35.1

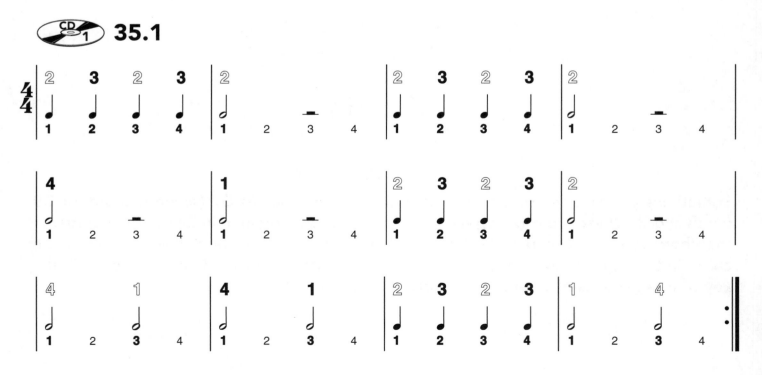

Once you are confident you can instantly find the root notes of chords $\bar{\text{I}}$, $\overline{\text{IV}}$ and $\overline{\text{V}}$, try playing through a 12 bar Blues using mainly root notes but using occasional other notes as well. This is demonstrated in the following examples. As your playing develops, you will be able to move freely between many different notes and use the root notes as landmarks to come back to when you want to emphasise them.

TONE DEVELOPMENT

One of the most important aspects of learning to play any instrument is the development of a strong, consistent tone. You can often tell the difference between a good player and an average player by hearing them play a slow simple melody and listening to their tone. A good player can really make their instrument sing and make a simple melody sound very moving. As you play the examples in the book, imagine you are singing the melody through your instrument and pay particular attention to your tone. Try playing at various dynamic levels (volumes). If you have trouble maintaining a strong, even tone at all volumes, practice playing long notes (at least 4 beats) on each of the holes of the harmonica at a slow tempo. In time you will notice a marked improvement in the consistency of your tone.

PLAYING BY EAR

The harmonica is great for playing slow plaintive melodies such as the following song **Shenandoah**. You probably already know the sound of this melody and other folk melodies. It is important to work on playing such melodies by ear. Listen to the recording and sing along with the harmonica until you have the melody in your memory, then work on reproducing it on the harmonica. Make a habit of doing this with as many melodies as possible. Developing the ability to play by ear will help you in a number of ways. It will enable you to respond quickly to what other musicians are playing and will help you develop a repertoire.

 37.0   **Shenandoah**

 37.1

This 12 bar Blues is a good exercise for building a strong, consistent tone. It contains a quick $\overline{\text{IV}}$ in the second bar. Learn it from memory and listen to the tone as you play.

RIFFS

As you learnt in lesson 6, a **riff** is a short repeating pattern which may be altered to fit various chord changes. Riffs are very common in Blues. The following riff uses eighth notes on the first two beats of bars 1 and 2, and then on all four beats of bar 3. Take it slowly at first and make sure you are sounding all of the notes clearly and evenly.

 **38.0**

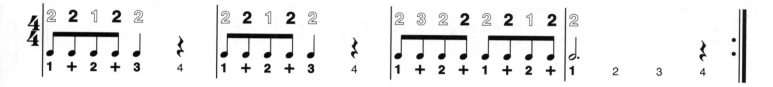

 **38.1**

In this example, the previous riff is altered to fit the changes of a 12 bar Blues progression As you learn new notes and rhythms, make a habit of inventing your own riffs based on everything you learn. You should also start copying riffs you hear on CDs featuring harmonica players. This is difficult at first, but the more you do it, the easier it gets. Build up a collection of riffs you can play from memory. Each one will teach you something new and the more riffs you know, the more versatile your playing will be.

54

Here is a riff which features eighth rests on the first and fourth beats. Once again, if you have trouble with the rhythm, clap it while counting out loud and then try playing the rhythm on one note. On the recording, the harmonica is omitted when the example repeats, leaving space for you to play the riff with the band.

 **39.0**

39.1

This example takes the previous riff and expands it to fit the 12 bar Blues progression. Notice that the basic rhythm is a repeating two bar pattern; i.e. the rhythm stays the same throughout the progression, only the pitches of the notes change.

Riffs are used in many styles of music and can be played with many other chord progressions as well as a 12 bar Blues. Here are some more riffs for you to learn. Each one is played once on the recording and then a space is left for you to play it with the band when the example repeats. As you make up new riffs, try them with the Jam-along tracks at the end of CD2 (page 178). As well as being enjoyable, this will help you develop the ability to play with a good time feel and prepare you for playing with a band.

40.0   Rock Riff

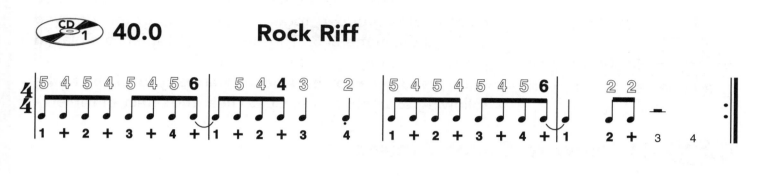

40.1   Country Rock Riff

40.2   Third Position Riff and Variation

This example consists of a four bar riff and a variation in the following four bars. It is played in Third position, which is described in detail in lesson 20. Don't worry about the description for now, just learn the riff and then create your own variations on it. Try this one with The Third position Jam-along track at the end of CD2 (ex82).

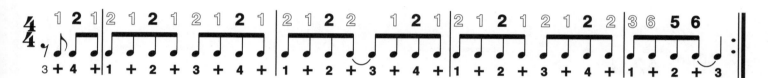

LESSON NINE

THE TRIPLET

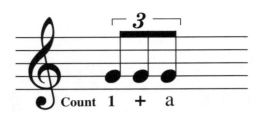

Count 1 + a

An eighth note **triplet** is a group of **three** evenly spaced notes played within one beat. Triplets are indicated by three eighth notes grouped together by a bracket (or a curved line) and the numeral **3**. The eighth note triplets are played with one third of a beat each. Triplets are easy to understand once you have heard them played. Listen to the following example on the CD to hear the effect of triplets.

 41 **How to Count Triplets**

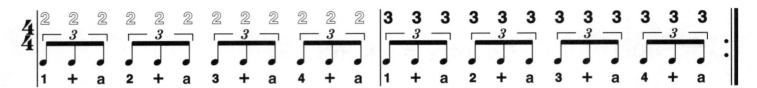

 42.0

Here is a triplet variation on the Blues riff you learnt in lesson 6. This one is played **cross harp in the key of G**.

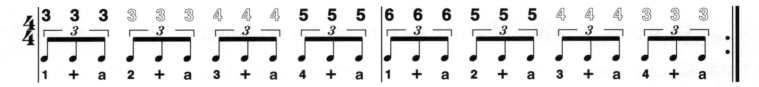

 **42.1**

This one is a Blues intro riff also played cross harp in the key of G. Listen to how effectively this triplet rhythm works with the other instruments. Once again, the harp is removed on the repeat to leave space for you to play with the rest of the band.

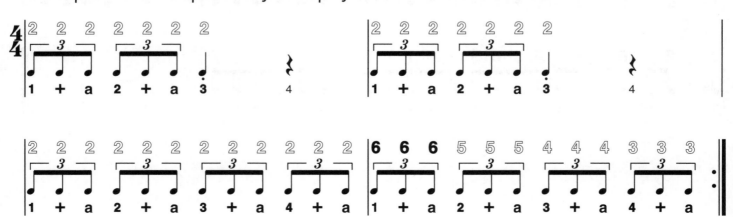

SWING RHYTHMS

A **swing rhythm** can be created by playing only the first and third notes of a triplet. Play the following example which contains a triplet on the second beat.

This example has the first and second notes of the triplet group tied. This gives the example a swing feel.

 **43.0**

The two eighth note triplets tied together in the previous example can be replaced by a quarter note.

 **43.1**

To simplify notation, it is common to replace the ♪♪ with ♪ ♪, and to write at the start of the piece ♪♪ = ♪ ♪ as illustrated below in example 43.2.

 **43.2**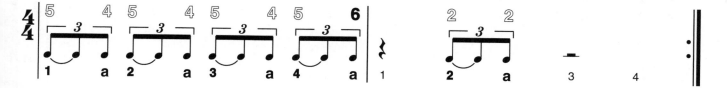

THE SHUFFLE

By using a constant stream of swinging eighth notes, an effect known as the **shuffle** is produced. The following example contains the now familiar cross harp Blues riff played as a shuffle.

 **44.0**

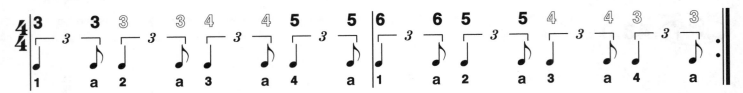 **44.1**

Here is the above riff extended to a full 12 bar Blues progression.

45.

Here is the same riff played in first position in the key of C. You have already learnt this exercise using straight eighth notes (ex23.1 - page 36). Notice the difference in feeling between this version and the earlier one.

46.   Battle Hymn of the Republic

This famous song can also be played with a shuffle feel. Try it with other songs as well.

LESSON TEN

SLIDING BETWEEN NOTES

Another common harmonica technique is to slide up or down to a specific note. This can really add drama and excitement to your playing. The symbol for a slide is a letter **S** above the note to which you are sliding, as shown here. Listen to the following example on the CD to hear the effect created by the use of slides. Once again the harp is omitted on the repeat so you can play with the band.

47.0

47.1

Here is a riff which makes use of slides. Once again, remember to swing the eighth notes.

THE TRAIL-OFF

There is another effect called a trail off which is the reverse of the slide. A trail-off is achieved by playing a note and then sliding away to an indefinite pitch. This technique is used on many instruments and is sometimes called a fall-off or a glissando. A trail-off is indicated by a wavy line moving down from the note to which it applies, as shown in the following example.

48.

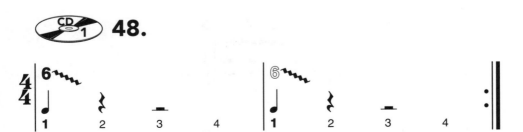

Here is a simple 12 bar Blues in the key of G demonstrating both slides and trail offs. Practice it slowly with a metronome until you can play the whole thing without losing your timing when sliding between notes, then play it along with the recording.

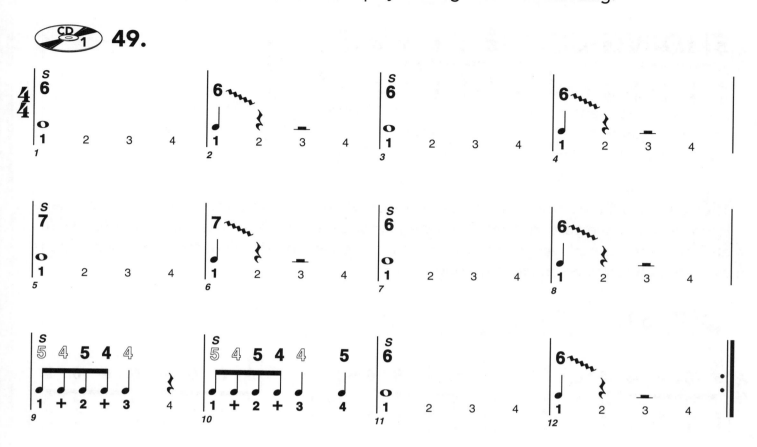

Here are some more riffs featuring slides and trail-offs. The harp has been omitted from the recording on the repeats so you can practice these techniques with the band. Once you have control of them, try adding these techniques to other riffs and melodies.

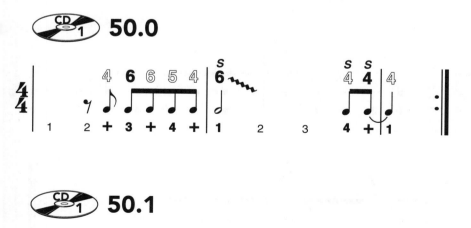

50.2

This one makes use of both slides and trail-offs.

The following Blues solo makes use of most of the rhythms and techniques you have learnt so far. Once you are confident using syncopated rhythms and techniques like slides and trail-offs, your playing will sound more expressive. As with all techniques, these things are most effective when used sparingly.

51.

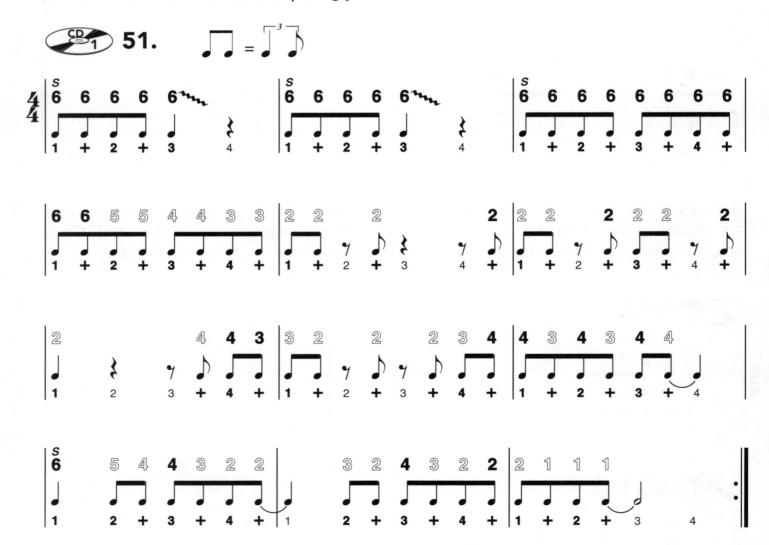

LESSON ELEVEN

BENDING NOTES

One of the most exciting sounds in harmonica playing is the use of note bending. This technique can be difficult at first and may take several months to gain control of, but is essential for Blues playing, so it is definitely worth developing. The most common bends are the **inhale** notes on the low end of the harmonica, from 1 to 6. It is also possible to bend exhale notes on the high end of the harmonica. However, this is a more advanced technique and is not dealt with here. To bend a note, the **back of your tongue** (not the tip) needs to move **up and back** to the back of your mouth. This changes the flow of air, resulting in the note "bending" **downwards to a lower pitch**. A good way to get the right feel for the movement required for bending notes is to say the word **Yo**, or **Yaw**. Another useful exercise to prepare you for bending is to **whistle a descending major scale**. As you do this, notice how the the back of your tongue moves back towards your throat as the pitch gets lower.

 52.0

This example demonstrates a half step bend on the inhale note of hole 4, as indicated by the letter **B** above the note. Everyone has trouble with bending at first and many people can't do it at all when they begin, so be patient and keep at it. In time, your perseverance will definitely pay off.

 **52.1**

Here is an exercise to help you gain control of note bending. Listen carefully as you play and keep the notes even.

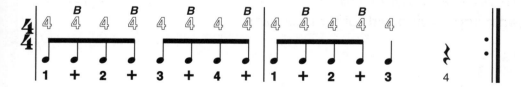

LICKS

Now try this Blues lick which makes use of the note bend you have just learnt. A **lick** is a short musical phrase which can be used as a basis for improvisation or joined with other licks to form a solo. Play along with the harp the first time through and then try it on your own for the repeat.

53.0

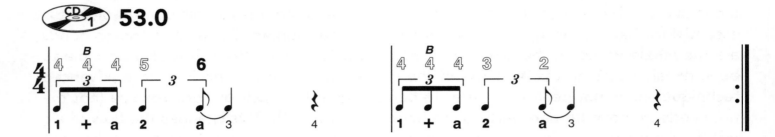

Here are some more licks which make use of the note bend on 4. Try inventing some of your own.

53.1

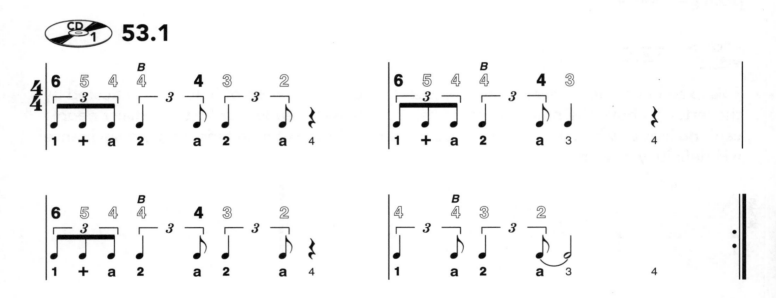

53.2

Once again, the harp is omitted on the repeat for you to play the lick with the band. Once you can play it correctly, try using the notes and rhythms to create your own variations. When you can do this, you will be ready to begin improvising with other musicians.

53.3

As with the previous example, learn this lick and then make up your own variations to play with the recording.

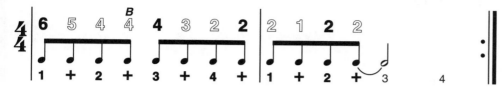

MORE NOTES TO BEND

Once you can bend the 4 note, try moving to holes 5 and 6 and bending these notes too. These are also half step bends and like the 4 bend, they may be difficult at first. The following example demonstrates these two bends.

 **54.0**

 54.1

Here is an exercise to help you gain control of all three of the bends you have learnt. Once again, listen carefully as you play and keep the notes even. If you are not sure of the notes you are bending to, listen to the example on the CD and then try to copy it.

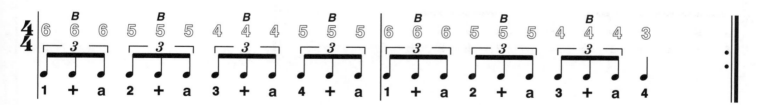

 **54.2**

Here is a Blues lick which makes use of bends on holes 4, 5 and 6.

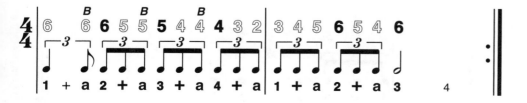

If you bend notes on hole 3, there are two possibilities instead of one. One of these is a **half step bend** and the other is a **whole step bend** which is a lower pitch than the first bend. A whole step bend is indicated by a line above the letter **B** ($\bar{B}$)The following example demonstrates both these bends.

 **55.0**

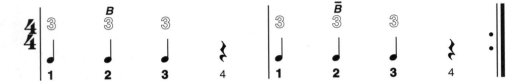

 **55.1**

Here is a lick which makes use of half step bends on hole 3.

 **55.2**

This one uses whole step bends on hole 3.

 **56.0**

Here is a lick which makes use of both bends on hole 3 along with the bend on 4.

The next bend you will learn is another whole step bend, this time on hole 2. Like hole 3, there are two possible bends available here, but the half step bend is rarely used. Listen to the CD to hear the correct pitch to bend to.

 **56.1**

 **56.2**

This exercise should help you gain control of the whole step bend on 2. This is one of the most difficult bends, so be patient with it and as with any other technique or lick you find difficult, practice it often but only for a short period each time.

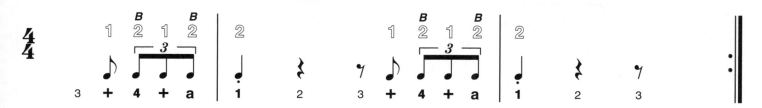

 **56.3**

This riff makes use of the 2 bend, but this time you will need to land directly on the bent note instead of hearing the natural 2 pitch first. This may take some time to master, but produces a great sound so keep at it. This riff uses a common Blues technique known as **call and response**, which as a question and answer style of playing either between two instruments or an instrument and vocal.

 **56.4**

Here is a common variation on the previous riff, this time using the half step bend on hole 3.

STOP TIME

The two previous riffs are commonly used in what is known as **stop time**. This involves the band playing a repeated riff with regular stops as part of the pattern. Either the singer or the soloist can play in the gaps between the stops. In the following solo, the band plays stop time for the first four bars and the harmonica plays a response in between each stop. In the fourth bar, the whole band plays a buildup which leads to the groove used for the rest of the progression. The groove used here was made famous by **Muddy Waters** in his song "Hoochie Coochie Man". This solo also features grace notes (indicated by a **w** above the indicated note. Grace notes are explained in detail on the following page.

 57. **Muddy's Rhythm**

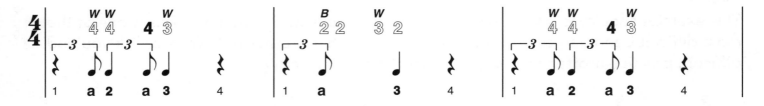

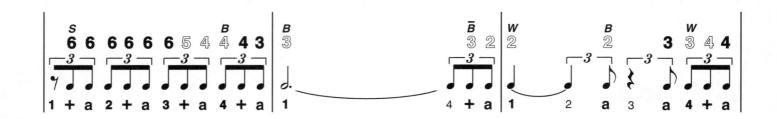

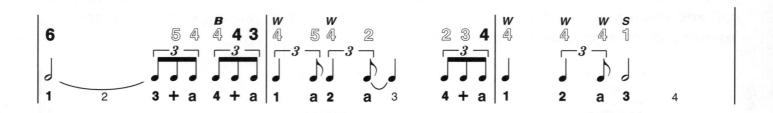

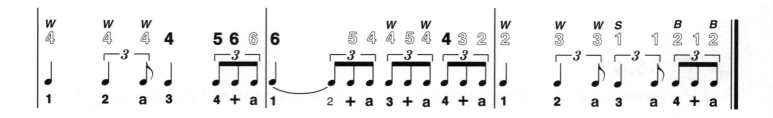

LESSON TWELVE

GRACE NOTES

Sometimes, instead of holding a note for its full value, you can start on a note (e.g. a bent note) and immediately move to another note. These very quick notes are called grace notes. Bent grace notes can be thought of as a **wah** sound produced by the mouth. The "**w**" is the grace note and the "**ah**" is the following note held for its usual length of time. Bent grace notes are indicated in the notation by the letter **W** above the note to which it applies.

58.0

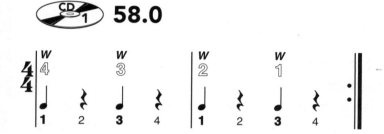

Here are some licks which make use of grace notes. Take them slowly at first and try to memorize each one.

58.1

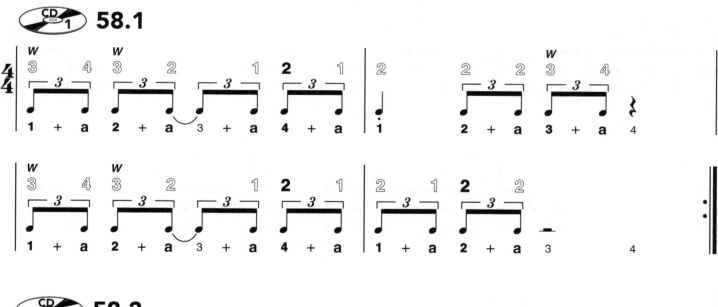

58.2

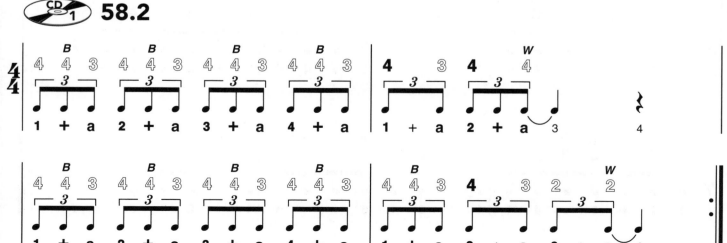

 **58.3**

Here is another lick containing both slide and bending grace notes.

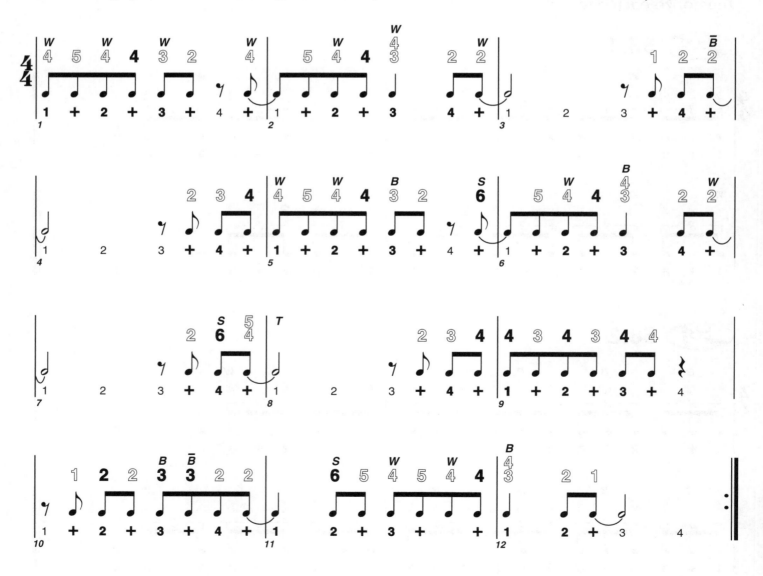

59 **Bending the Blues**

This 12 bar Blues in the key of G sums up all of the techniques presented in the lesson. It also contains double stops (2 notes played together). Listen to the CD and try to copy all the sounds you hear. Then try to memorize the solo one lick at a time. A great way to memorise something is to learn to sing it. First, listen to the CD many times and try to imitate the harmonica part using sounds close to the ones made by the harmonica (**wah**, **ta**, etc). Then try singing the harmonica part without the CD. Once you can sing something, you have it well in your memory and should find it a lot easier to play.

THE TRILL

Another exciting sound often played on the harmonica is the **trill**. A trill is a rapid alternation between two inhaled notes or two exhaled notes. This can be achieved either by rapidly moving the harmonica from side to side while maintaining a steady breath, or by rolling the head from side to side while holding the harmonica steady. Both these methods are common in harmonica playing. A trill is indicated by two holes (eg. $\frac{5}{4}$) with the symbol *Tr* written above them.

60.0

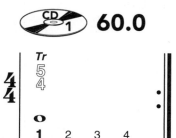

When you begin learning the trill, you may have trouble getting the notes to sound clearly and evenly. Here is an exercise which should help. Take it slowly at first.

60.1

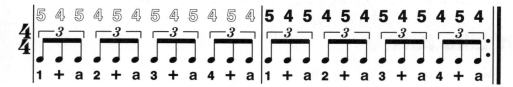

60.2

Here is a typical Blues lick using the trill on holes 4 and 5.

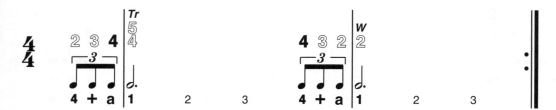

60.3

Here is a variation. The rhythm is exactly the same as the previous example, but the notes have been changed. The trill here is between holes 3 and 4.

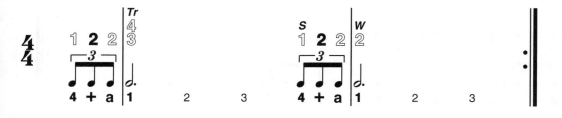

THROAT VIBRATO

Another sound commonly used by harmonica players is **throat vibrato**. This is another way of adding expression to a note once it has sounded. The sound is made with a similar movement to both laughing and coughing. Try saying ha ha ha ha very quickly as you breath in. Then try it breathing out. Then try the same thing as you play a note on the harmonica. Listen to the CD to hear the effect produced by throat vibrato. Like note bending, this technique can take some time to master, so be patient and stick with it. Throat vibrato is indicated by the symbol ⌁ placed after the hole number.

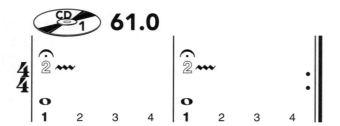

61.0

To finish this section, here is a Blues solo which makes use of all the techniques you have learnt. Take it slowly at first and listen carefully to the CD to get all the expressions. Once you can play this one, you are well on the way to being a good Harmonica player. Make a habit of improvising with the Jam-along tracks at the end of CD2. The progressions are described on page 178. As well as this, you should start playing regularly with other musicians.

61.1   **Tell It Like It Is**

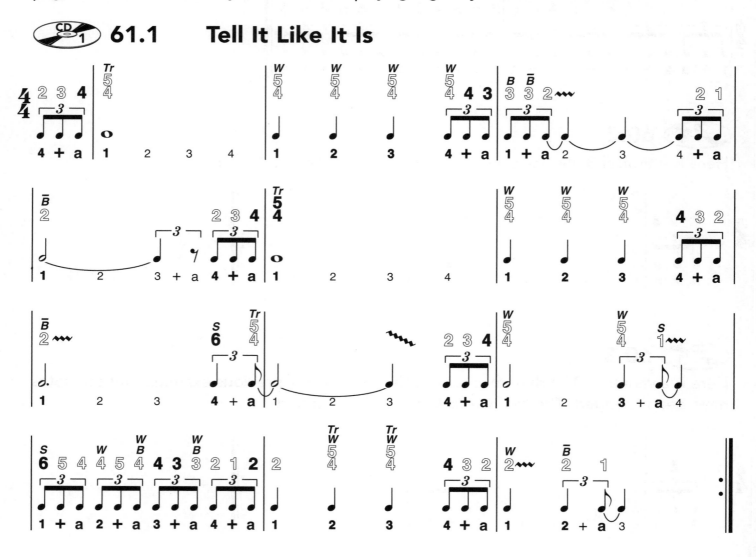

SECTION 3
Sixteenth Note Rhythms, Understanding Notes, Scales and Keys, 3rd and 4th Positions

LESSON THIRTEEN

SIXTEENTH NOTES

 This is a **sixteenth note**.
It lasts for **one quarter** of a beat.
There are **four** sixteenth notes in one beat.
There are **16** sixteenth notes in one bar of
4/4 time.

Four sixteenth notes joined together.

Count: 1   e   +   a
Say: one   'ee'   and   'ah'

62 How to Count Sixteenth Notes

Tap your foot on each beat and count mentally as you play.

Now try this example which contains sixteenth notes moving between two different notes. On the recording, the harp has been omitted on the repeat for you to play with the band.

63.0

63.1

This one uses 16th notes moving between three different notes. Learn it carefully and then play along with the recording.

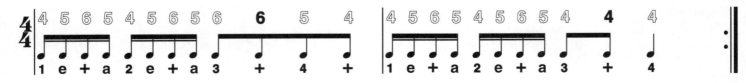

A good way to gain control of any new rhythm or beat subdivision (in this case 16th notes) is to use it to play scales and sequences you are familiar with. This way you can concentrate solely on the timing. The following example demonstrates the C Major scale played in quarter, eighth and sixteenth notes. Practice it slowly with a metronome and tap your foot on each beat as you play. As you change between the subdivisions, remember that the notes get faster, but the beat remains in exactly the same place regardless of the subdivisions.

 64.0

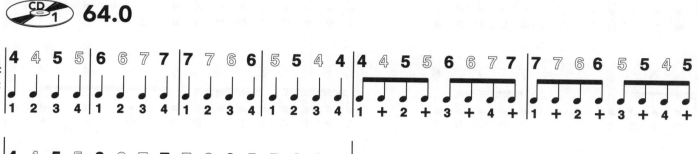

Once you are comfortable playing the scale in 16th notes, try playing some sequences using 16ths as shown here. Play slowly and evenly with a metronome, then gradually increase the tempos once you can do it perfectly.

 64.1

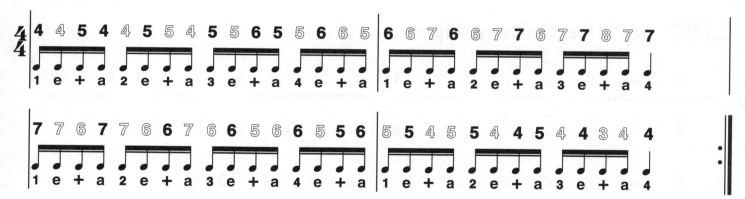

 64.2

Now try the following melodies which feature sixteenth notes along with other note values you learnt earlier in the book.

 **65 Rolling Along**

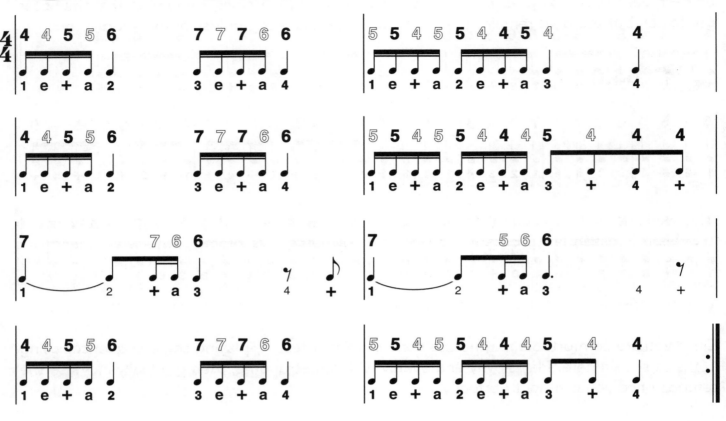

 **66 The Galway Piper**

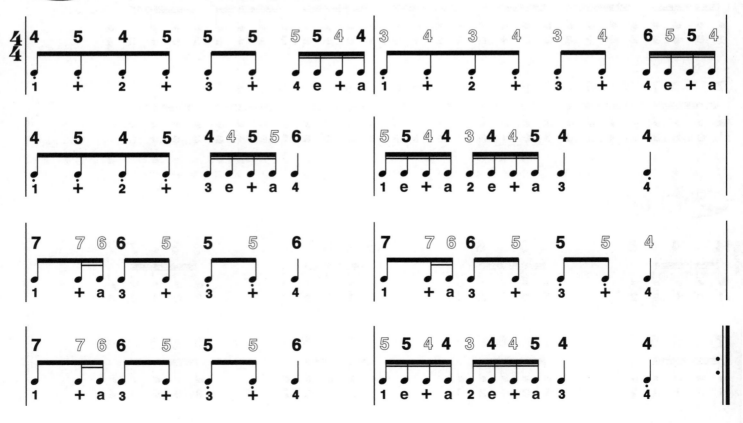

Often in songs you will find two sixteenth notes grouped together with an eighth note. The following example will help you gain control of these groupings.

67.

68 Arkansas Traveller

This well known American folk song is sounds best when played quite fast, but before you try this it is essential to be able to play it with the correct timing, otherwise it loses it's effectiveness. Take it very slowly at first and only increase the tempo (speed) when you can confidently play all the notes cleanly and evenly. Practice it with a metronome and increase the tempo a couple of notches at a time until you can play it with the recording.

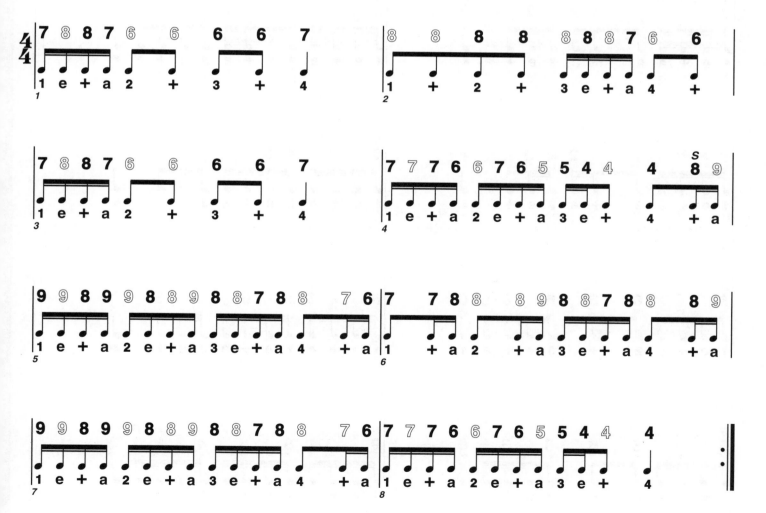

Sixteenth notes are great for playing train rhythms, as demonstrated in the following example. Take this one slowly at first and tap your foot on each beat to help you keep time.

69.

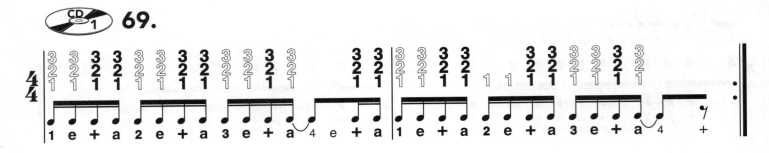

70 Cross Country

This Country flavored cross harp solo is a real challenge. It contains many sixteenth notes along with bends and grace notes using bends and slides. Listen to the CD and learn it one lick at a time if you have trouble with it.

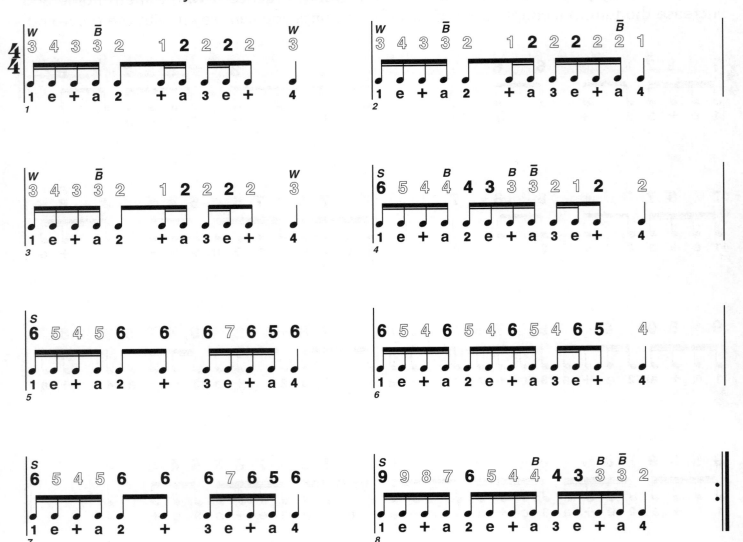

LESSON FOURTEEN

DOTTED EIGHTH NOTES

Another common sixteenth note timing is when a sixteenth note is played after a dotted eighth note, i.e.

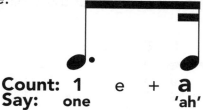

Count: **1**   e   +   **a**
Say: one   'ah'

The dot placed after the eighth note lengthens the note by half its value. The dotted eighth note is equivalent in duration to three sixteenth notes, i.e.

 **71.0**

This example demonstrates the rhythm shown above. Play it slowly with a metronome and tap your foot on each beat.

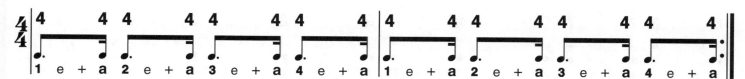

71.1   **Here Comes the Bride**

Here is a traditional wedding song which makes frequent use of this rhythm.

THE SIXTEENTH REST

This is a **sixteenth rest**.
It indicates **a quarter of a beat of silence**.

72 The Gypsy Rover

This folk song contains several sixteenth rests. Listen to the CD if you are unsure of the timing.

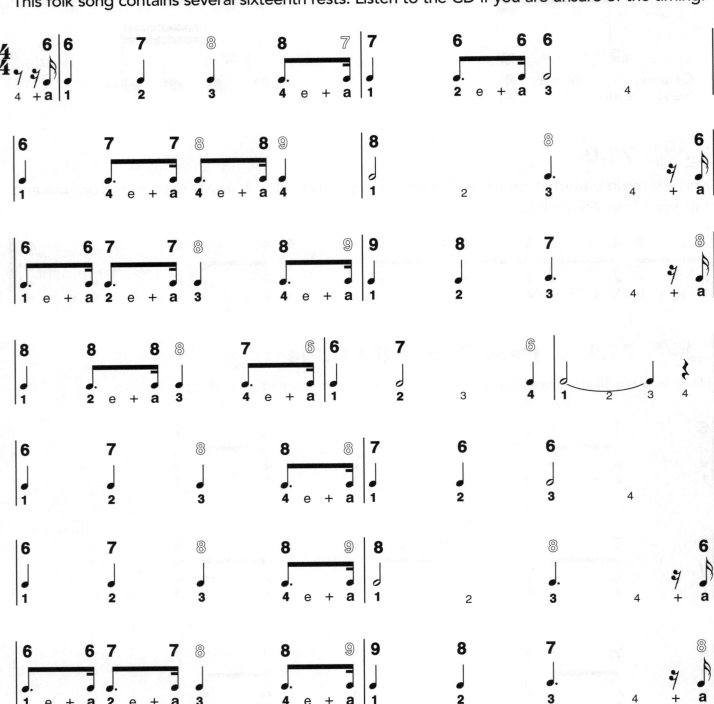

Sometimes you will find the figure reversed, i.e. a sixteenth note followed by a dotted eighth note, as shown below. This is the reverse of the figure you learnt on page 79.

Count: 1   e   +   a
Say: one   ee

 **73.**

Listen to the CD to hear the effect produced by this rhythm. Once again, count silently as you play. An easy way to learn this figure is to think of it as two sixteenth notes with the second one sustained up to the following beat.

Here is a song which uses the above rhythm as well as the dotted eighth note followed by a sixteenth note. Listen to the CD if you are unsure of the timing and then practice it slowly until you can play it from memory.

74   **Ten Green Bottles**

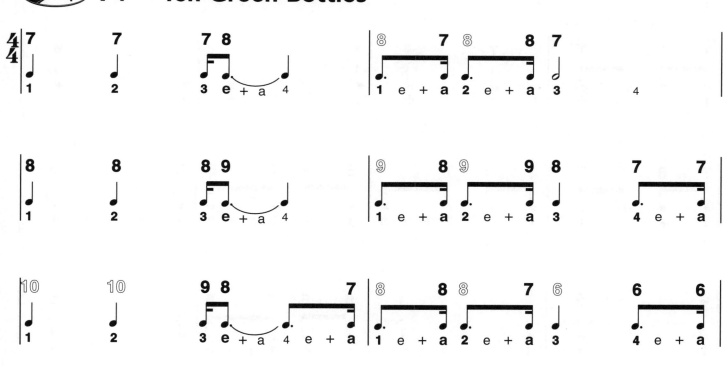

THE TWO FOUR TIME SIGNATURE

2/4 The 2/4 time signature tells you that there are only two quarter note beats in one bar. The only difference between 2/4 and 4/4 is that in 2/4 time there are twice as many bar lines.

FIRST AND SECOND ENDINGS

The following song contains **first and second endings**. The **first** time you play through the song, play the **first ending** (⌐1.⌐), then go back to the beginning. The **second** time you play through the song, play the **second ending** (⌐2.⌐) instead of the first.

 **75 Dixie**

SIXTEENTH NOTES AND TIES

You already know how to interpret rhythms using ties with whole, half, quarter and eighth notes. Sixteenth note rhythms involving ties can be difficult to play at first, so it is worth practicing them on one note until you have control of them. In the following example there are several ties between the last of a group of four sixteenth notes (the "**a**" count) and the note on the next beat. Count and clap the rhythm several times until you understand it, and then play the example.

 **76.0**

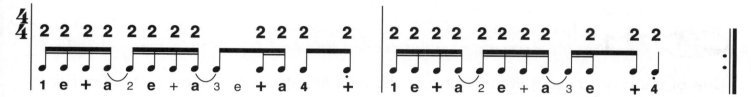

 **76.1**

Here is a solo making use of ties in this manner. The same rhythm repeats several times, so once you have control of it in the first line, the rest should be easy. This solo has a minor key sound and is played in **third position** which is the subject of lesson 20.

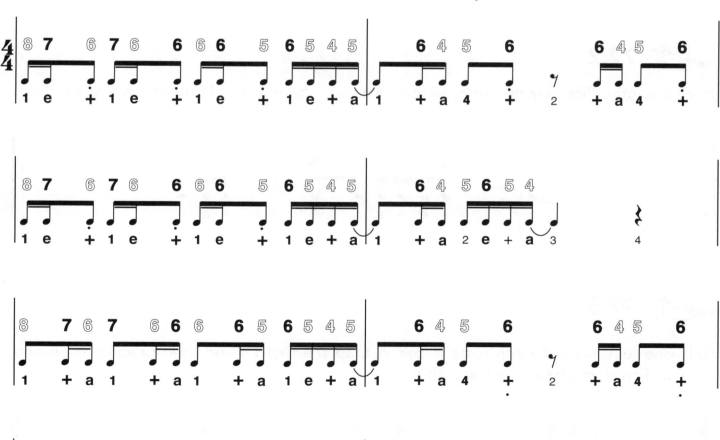

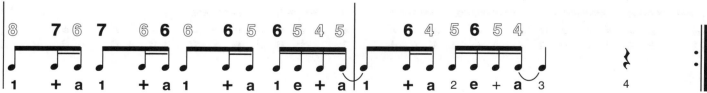

Another common rhythm figure is a sixteenth note followed by an eighth note and then another sixteenth, as shown in bar two of the following example.

77.0

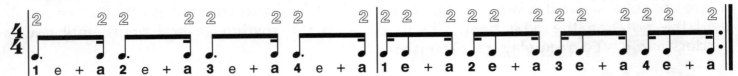

77.1

One of the ways these rhythms can be used is to imitate horn section parts, particularly when playing R&B and Funk.

77.2

Here is another lick making use of sixteenth notes. This one also features a trill and a slide.

77.3

This one features sixteenth rests in bar 2. Clap the rhythm and then practice it on one note at first if you have trouble with it.

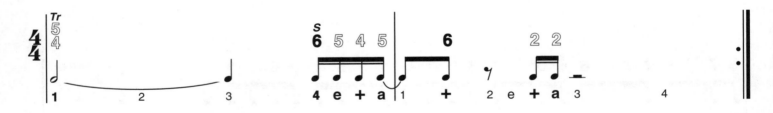

To finish this lesson, here is a solo which is based on sixteenth notes. Take your time with this one, as it may be difficult at first. Listen to the CD to hear the timing and all the expressions. As suggested earlier, clap any rhythms you have trouble with while counting out loud and tapping your foot on each beat. Once again the harp has been omitted on the repeat so you can play the whole solo with the band.

78 Twistin' and Turnin'

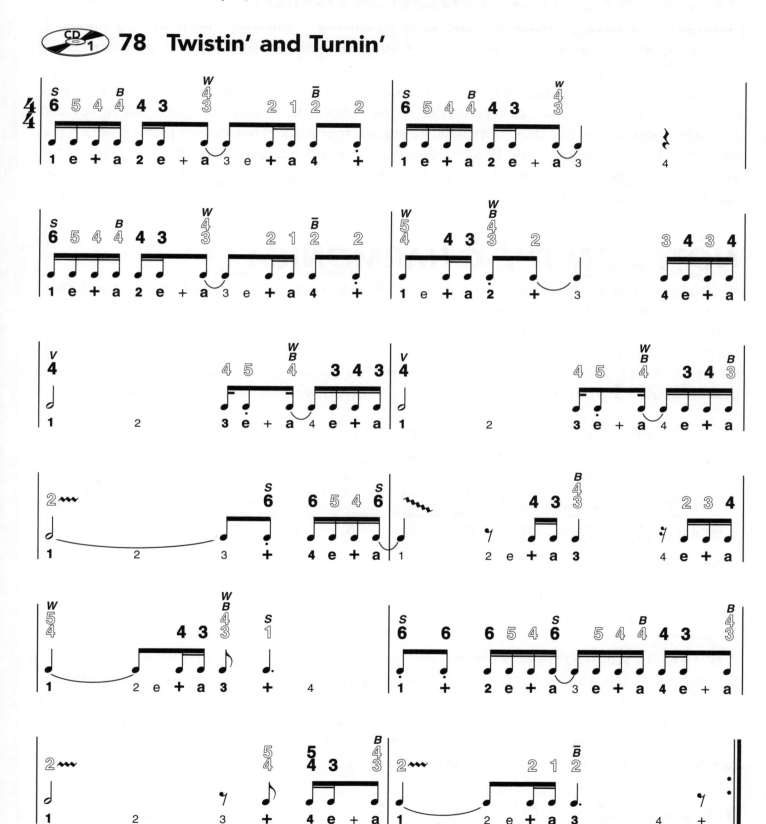

LESSON FIFTEEN

WHAT ARE ALL THESE SOUNDS?

Through the course of the book you have learnt many different notes in two different playing positions (first position and second position or cross harp). There are various musical ways of describing all these notes and relating them to keys. There are two different ways to approach this lesson. You may wish to study each scale and description in detail, or you may wish to use it basically as a reference while continuing to develop your playing by ear and asking questions of other musicians. There are many good harmonica players who have very little knowledge of music theory. However, it is the author's belief that you can get a lot further if you understand the sounds you are making and how to transfer them to harmonicas in other keys.

NOTES ON THE C HARMONICA

The following diagram shows the names of all of the notes you have learnt in the book. There are technically a few more possible notes you could find on the C harmonica, particularly by bending the higher exhale notes, but these have been omitted to keep the diagram as simple as possible. The symbol ♭ beside some of the notes is a **flat sign**. Flat means a lower pitch. By using these signs it is possible to indicate pitches halfway between letter names, e.g. the note **D♭** is halfway between the notes **C** and **D**.

Exhale	C	E	G	C	E	G	C	E	G	C
	1	2	3	4	5	6	7	8	9	10
Inhale	D	G	B	D	F	A	B	D	F	A
Bend	D♭	F	B♭ or A	D♭	E	A♭				

If you wish to study harmonica playing seriously, it is worth taking some time to memorize the names of the notes on the harmonica along with their **scale degrees** which measure the distance of each note from the key note (in this case, **C**). The **key** is the central note which all the other notes relate to. Since there are seven different notes in the major scale, each note can be given a number from 1 to 7 as shown below. When the number 8 is reached, the pattern begins again, since 8 is a repeat of 1 an octave higher.

Note Name	C	D	E	F	G	A	B	C
Scale Degree	1	2	3	4	5	6	7	8

Once you know how to bend notes, it is possible to play a lower octave of the C major scale starting on hole **1**, as demonstrated in the following example. This is a great exercise for gaining control of note bending. As you play this scale, listen carefully to the pitch of each of the bent notes to make sure they are in tune.

 **79.0**

Once you can play the scale in quarter notes, try playing it a bit faster. This example demonstrates the low octave without bends and then the full scale with bends.

 **79.1**

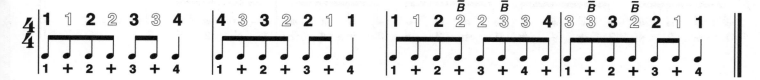

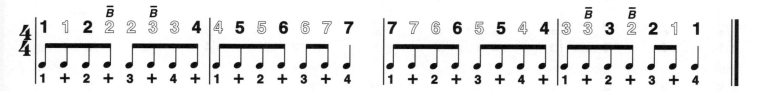 **79.2**   **Two Octave C Major Scale**

Once you have control of the low octave of C major, add it to the middle octave which you already know.

COMPLETE RANGE OF THE HARMONICA

If you try playing the highest octave of the C major scale starting on hole **7**, you will find that the note **B** (the **7th** degree) is missing, so you get C (1), D (2), E (3), F (4), G (5), A (6) C (8). The following example contains three octaves of the C major scale (apart from the missing B note), which is the complete range of the C harmonica. **All** ten hole diatonic harmonicas have a range of 3 octaves regardless of what key they are tuned to. When you play in the key written on the harmonica (in this case **C**) instead of cross harp, you are playing in **first position**. As you learnt in lesson 2, **cross harp** is often referred to as **second position**.

79.3

As you play this example, try to mentally name the notes as you play. If you have trouble, think do, re, mi at first, then name the notes. Once you can do this, play it again and mentally sing the scale degrees as you play. Remember that the octave of C (degree 8) is equal to degree 1, so count each new C as a **1** rather than an **8**. E.g. **1,2,3,4,5,6,7,1,2,3,4,5,6,7,1,2,3**, etc. It is important to remember that scale degrees are purely theoretical numbers which relate to all instruments regardless of their playing techniques. Do not confuse scale degrees with the numbers of the holes on the harmonica.

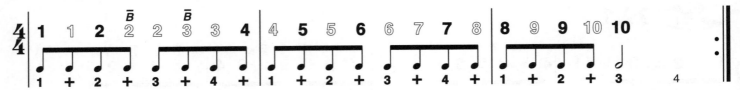

80   The Springtime it Brings on the Shearing

This melody is played right at the top of the harmonica. Learn it and then analyze the degrees. If you make a habit of this, you will learn new melodies much quicker.

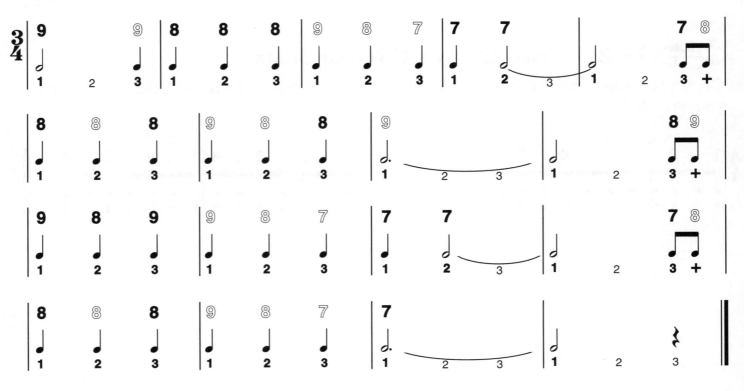

THE MAJOR PENTATONIC SCALE

You will have noticed that in order to play the low octave of the C major scale, it was necessary to produce some extra notes by bending. Also, in the high octave, the note **B** was missing. This is because of the way the harmonica is tuned. It is possible to create melodies without all of the notes of the major scale. In fact, the major scale is only one of many different scales used in music. By leaving out the **4th** and **7th** degrees of the major scale, the major pentatonic scale is created. As the name suggests, pentatonic scales contain only five different notes. There are many melodies, particularly in folk and gospel music which are derived from the major pentatonic scale. One you have already learnt is *Swing Low, Sweet Chariot*. Others include *Amazing Grace* and *Tom Dooley*. The C major pentatonic scale is shown below.

C Major Pentatonic

C	D	E	G	A	C
1	2	3	5	6	8(1)

 **81.0**

Here is the C major pentatonic scale played in the middle octave. Once again, try mentally naming the scale degrees as you play.

Once you are comfortable playing the major pentatonic scale in the middle octave, try playing it over the full 3 octave range of the harmonica. As with the C major scale, you will need to bend hole 3 to obtain the **6th** degree of the scale (an **A** note) in the low octave.

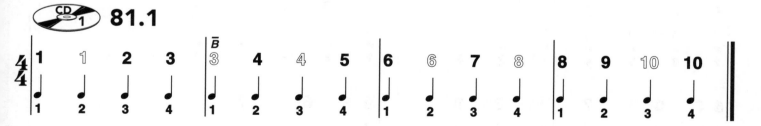 **81.1**

90

CD 1 82.0 **Amazing Grace**

CD 1 82.1 **Tom Dooley**

LESSON SIXTEEN

CROSS HARP SOUNDS

When you play cross harp, you are playing in the key of **G**. This means that all the scale degrees for cross harp playing relate to the note G instead of C. To play the G major scale, the note **F sharp** is required. Just as a flat lowers the pitch of a note, a sharp (♯) raises the pitch of a note. This means that the note **F♯** is halfway between F and G. The note F♯ is not available on the C harmonica, which means the G major scale cannot be played on the C harmonica. However, the cross harp position is normally used for more bluesy sounds which do not use the major scale but do contain a **flattened 7th** degree. By flattening the 7th degree of the major scale, the **mixolydian** scale or mode is produced. A comparison of the G major scale and the G mixolydian scale is shown below.

G Major Scale

G	A	B	C	D	E	F♯	G
1	2	3	4	5	6	7	8

G Mixolydian Scale

G	A	B	C	D	E	♭7	G
1	2	3	4	5	6	F	8

83.

Here is the G mixolydian scale played first in the middle octave and then over two octaves. Notice the slightly mournful sound produced by the ♭7 degree. This is one of the sounds that makes cross harp so effective for Blues playing. As you play this example, mentally name the scale degrees, remembering that G is the keynote instead of C. The note G can be found at holes 2, 3, 6, and 9. The solo "**Cross Country**" which you learnt in lesson 13 uses the G mixolydian scale.

THE G MAJOR PENTATONIC SCALE

It is also possible to use the cross harp position to play the G major pentatonic. Remember that the major pentatonic scale is like a major scale with the 4th and 7th degrees omitted. Shown below is a comparison of the G mixolydian scale and the G major pentatonic scale.

G Mixolydian

G	A	B	C	D	E	F	G
1	2	3	4	5	6	♭7	8

G Major Pentatonic

G	A	B		D	E		G
1	2	3		5	6		8

 **84.**

Here is the G major pentatonic scale played over two octaves. Once again, mentally name the scale degrees as you play. Do this until you know which degree you are on as soon as you play it.

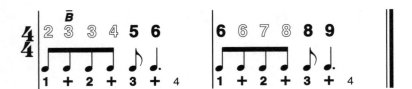

 **85** **Amazing Grace**

Here is the song Amazing Grace played cross harp in the key of G. All of the notes of this song come from the G major pentatonic scale. The bends from **B** to **A** on hole 3 can be tricky, so take care with them.

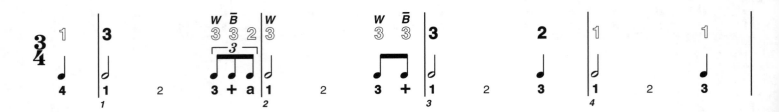

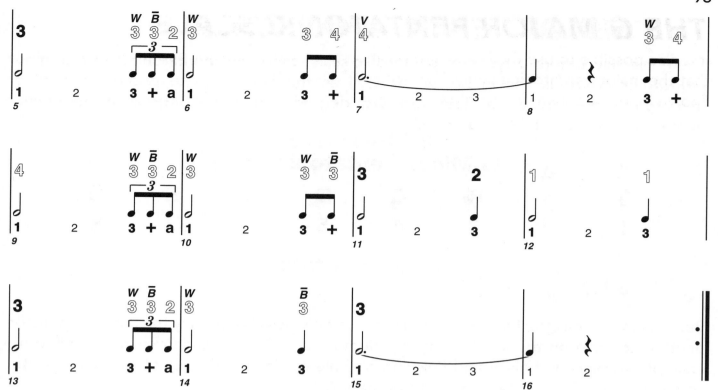

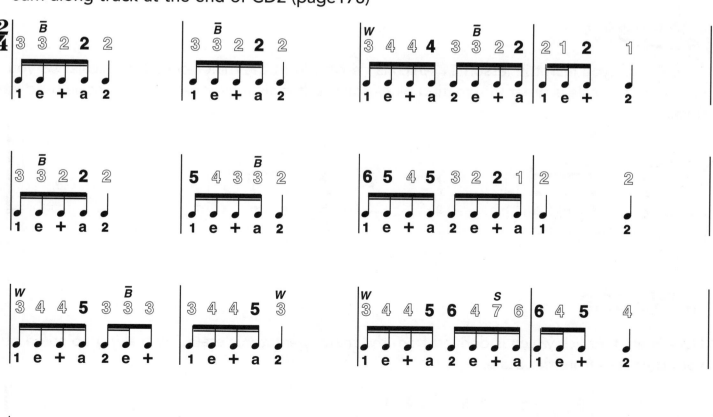

86. Cajun Two Step

Here is a more complex solo using the major pentatonic scale. Learn it and then try using the ideas to create your own licks from the scale as well as improvising with the Country Jam-along track at the end of CD2 (page178)

THE MINOR PENTATONIC SCALE

There are **two** different types of pentatonic scale, the major pentatonic and the **minor pentatonic** which is shown below. As well as the flattened 7th degree, the minor pentatonic also contains a **flattened 3rd** degree. The scale degrees of the minor pentatonic scale are **1**, ♭**3**, **4**, **5** and ♭**7**.

G Minor Pentatonic Scale

G	B♭	C	D	F	G
1	♭3	4	5	♭7	8

 **87.0**

Because of the way the harmonica is tuned, it is only possible to play the cross harp minor pentatonic scale on the low end of the harmonica. The scale is shown in the following example starting on hole 2 and finishing on hole 6, along with part of the scale on the very low notes down as far as the 4th degree (**C**).

 **87.1**

Here is a riff you learnt in lesson 11 which is derived from the minor pentatonic scale. As you can hear, this scale is great for creating Blues sounds. It is also the most common scale used in Rock.

 **87.2**

Here is another lick which is derived from the minor pentatonic scale. Try making up some of your own licks from this scale.

THE BLUES SCALE

By adding one extra note (the flattened fifth degree) to the minor pentatonic scale, the Blues scale is created. This scale is used by all instrumentalists to create Blues melodies.

G Blues Scale

G	B♭	C	D♭	D	F	G
1	♭3	4	♭5	5	♭7	8

 **88.0**

Like the minor pentatonic scale, the cross harp Blues scale can only be played on the low end of the harmonica. The G Blues scale is shown here along with a partial lower octave of the scale down as far as the 4th degree (**C**).

88.1

Here is a lick derived from the G Blues scale.

88.2

When improvising, it is common to use notes from all of the scales you have learnt. The following lick is made from a combination of the G mixolydian scale and the G Blues scale.

LESSON SEVENTEEN

ARTICULATIONS

There are many different ways in which a note can be played, e.g. loud, soft, staccato, legato, etc. These different ways of playing a note are called **articulations**. The way you articulate notes can make a dramatic difference to the way the music sounds. There are specific markings which can be used in written music to indicate the articulation desired by the composer. Two examples of this are shown below. A short horizontal line directly above or below a note indicates that the note is to be held for its full written duration. This articulation is called **tenuto**. Another common articulation which you may already know is **staccato**, which means the note is to be played short and separate from other notes. Staccato is indicated by a dot placed directly above or below a note.

Tenuto   **Staccato**

CD 1 **89.0**

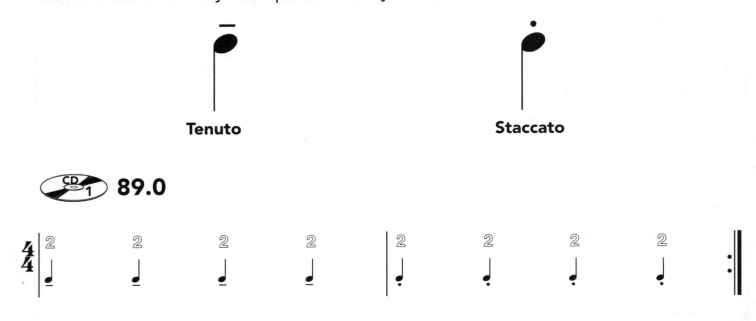

Most sheet music doesn't contain detailed articulation markings. Sometimes staccato notes are marked, but tenuto usually isn't. It is often assumed that most notes will be played tenuto (held for their written duration) The following example shows the G Blues scale alternating between tenuto (not indicated) and staccato. This is often described as long-short. Practice all your scales and in this manner until it becomes natural to you. Once you con do this, it will start to come out in your playing by itself.

CD 1 **89.1**

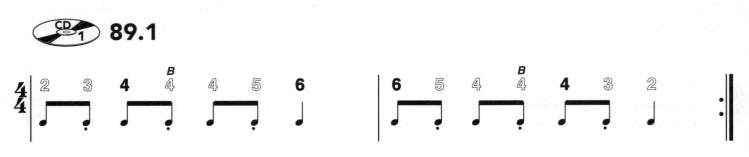

ACCENTS

Another important aspect of articulating notes is the use of **Accents**. Accent markings are used to indicate notes which are to be played louder than other notes. There are two common types of accents, these being a tenuto accent (long) and a staccato accent (short). The long accent is indicated by a horizontal wedge mark above or below the note. The short accent is indicated by a vertical wedge mark above or below the note.

Long accent   **Short Accent**

Listen to the recording to hear the difference between these two accents. Practice this exercise until you can do it easily and then work on playing the Blues scale with both types of accents, separately and then alternating. It is recommended that you do this with all the scales in the book in all positions. This way you will develop the ability to use accents naturally whenever you feel them.

90.0

Here is an example which uses both types of accents. Try adding accents to phrases you already know and then make a habit of using accents in your improvising.

90.1

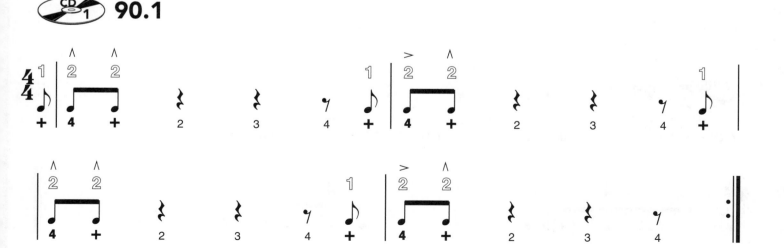

GHOST NOTES

A **ghost note** is the opposite of an accent. It is a note played softer than other notes. A ghost note is indicated by brackets placed either side of the note as shown below. The amount of "ghosting" is up to the individual player. A ghost note can be anything from about half the volume of unghosted notes right down to barely audible.

(𝅗𝅥) **Ghost Note** indicated by brackets

91.0

91.1

As with other expressions and articulations, it is a good idea to practice ghost notes with your scales and arpeggios. This example demonstrates the **G Blues scale** using ghost notes on the beat. Space has been left for you to play by yourself on the repeat.

91.2

Here is a riff which makes use of ghost notes off the beat instead of on the beat.

LEARNING FROM HORN PLAYERS

All the articulations you have learnt are also used by saxophone and trumpet players. The great Chicago Blues harp player **Little Walter** got many of his ideas by listening to sax players and horn sections. The following solo is in the style of Little walter and demonstrates how effectively a harp and guitar can imitate a horn section.

It is also important to listen carefully to the articulations used by harp players on your favorite albums and imitate the ones you like. All good players have worked on their articulation to help them express the music in a way that moves people. By studying their articulations, you will gain more control of them yourself and your own playing will become more expressive.

92. Juke Joint Jive

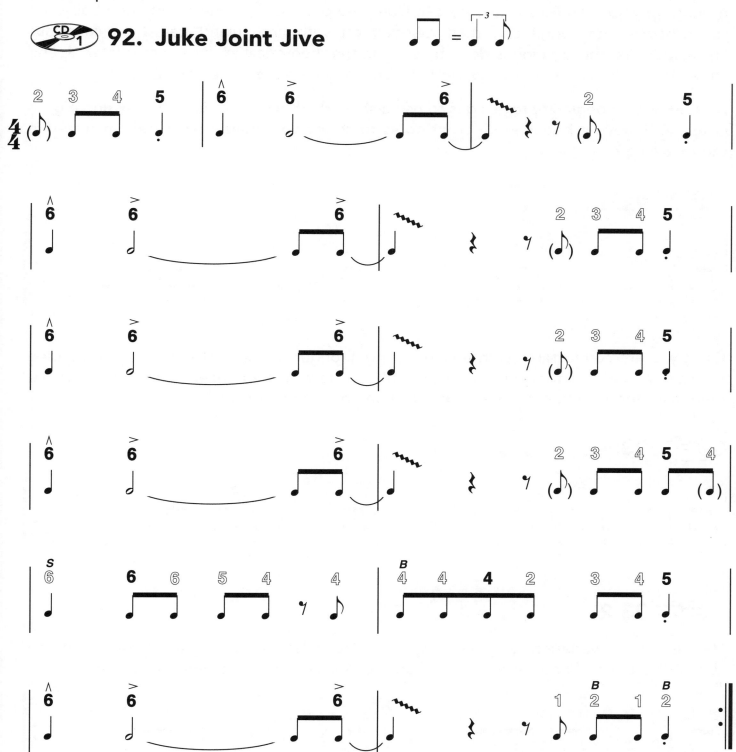

LESSON EIGHTEEN

IMPROVISATION

Improvisation means creating your own melodies by ear. You now know more than enough to begin improvising. Although some licks and melodies are derived entirely from one scale, it is also common that notes from a combination of scales is used. Most musicians create new melodies totally by ear, drawing on all the sounds they are familiar with. When you are learning, the best approach is to learn all the sounds and scales but also to experiment with making up your own licks totally by ear. Composing is usually done by intuition based on subconscious knowledge and then rounded off with fine tuning based on conscious knowledge, i.e. the creating is done by ear and the theoretical analysis comes later. Spend some time each day improvising over the Jam-along tracks at the end of CD2 (page 178).

A good way to begin improvising is to use a short rhythm pattern (e.g. two swung eighth notes) and move it between different notes to create variations. This is demonstrated in the following example.

93.0

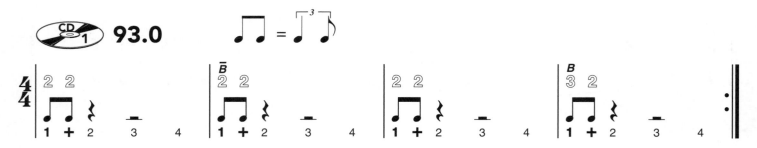

Once you are comfortable with this, try using a longer rhythm pattern. It is a good idea to play any new rhythm on one note until you have it memorized. This next example demonstrates a rhythm on one note and then on a variety of pitches.

93.1

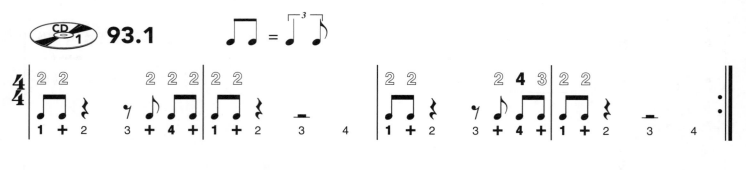

93.2

Here is another variation using a set rhythm pattern. Notice the way using the rhythm on different groups of notes creates a call and response effect between the phrases.

 **93.3**

This one uses a repetition and variation approach which is a common improvising technique. One of the most important things to remember when using the repetition and variation technique is to keep your basic idea fairly simple. This makes it easy to develop and easy for the listener to follow what you are doing.

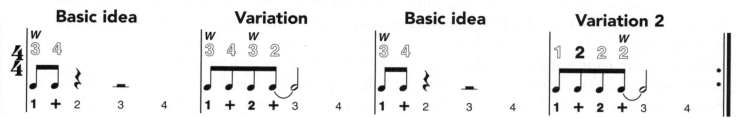

Another useful improvising technique is to begin with a short rhythmic phrase and then add longer variations, each one adding something to what has gone before.

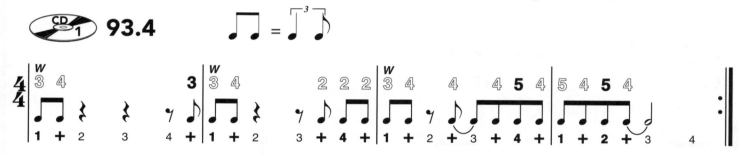

 **94.   Tell Me a Story**

Here is a Blues solo based on the previous example. Notice the use or repetition and variation throughout. A great player to listen to for this kind of improvisation is **Sonny Boy Williamson Ⅱ**. His real name was Rice Miller. There is also an earlier Sonnyboy Williamson.

THE TURNAROUND

In most Blues songs, each verse ends with what is called a **turnaround.** A turnaround is a way of setting the music up for a repeat, so that the listener is ready for the next verse or solo. Turnarounds commonly occur on the last two bars of the Blues progression. The chords found in the turnaround are usually $\bar{\text{I}}$ and $\underline{\text{V}}$. In the key of G the chords used in these two bars would be G or G7 and D or D7. Although you can use any of the notes of the Blues scale or a combination of scales to play over all the chords of a Blues progression, it is common to change some of the notes along with the chord changes, e.g. ending the phrase on the root note of the accompanying chord as shown in the following example, or using mostly notes contained in the chord. This is particularly important on the turnaround of a verse or solo. The first bar here is played over a G7 chord, so the harmonica plays the notes B and G which are both part of a G7 chord. In the second bar, the accompaniment plays a D7 chord and the harmonica plays an F from the G Blues scale and ends on a D note which is the root note of the D7 chord. Listen to how well these notes fit with the accompaniment.

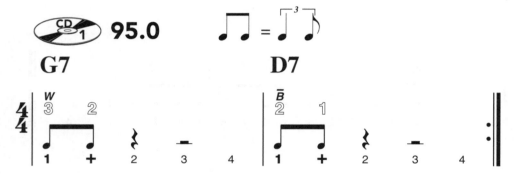

Here are some typical examples of the type of licks you might find on a Blues turnaround. Try making up some of your own, as well as listening to Blues albums for ideas to use on turnarounds.

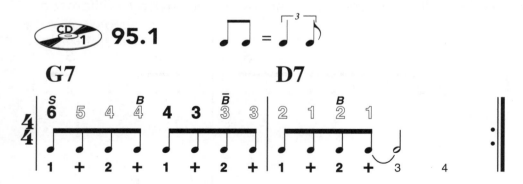

EAR TRAINING

Probably the most important aspect of harmonica playing is being able to play a melody by ear and respond to other musicians. Many people have trouble with this at first, but it is really just a matter of **listening**, **practice** and **patience**. All notes used in music can be written down and therefore have a specific pitch and time value. Through the course of this book you will learn the fundamentals of all of the common time values for notes as well as a method of identifying pitches and how they relate to other pitches in a song. The best way to start improving your ability to play "in time" and "in tune" is to copy the sounds made by someone else. The easiest way to do this is to play along with a recording and try to copy the harmonica player, or the vocal melody. Listen carefully to both the rhythms and the pitches. Here are some exercises to help you develop this ability. There is no notation for these examples, you simply copy what you hear on the recording. In example 96, the harmonica plays a rhythm using a G note in one bar and then you repeat it in the following bar.

 ## 96 Matching Rhythms   (hole 2e)

 ## 97   Matching Pitches

Now try matching the pitches played by the harmonica on this example. Once again, the harmonica plays in one bar and a space is left for you to repeat what you just heard in the next bar.

 ## 98 Matching Short Phrases (cross Harp)

This example contains short phrases using rhythm and a variety of pitches. As before, listen carefully and then copy what you hear. Do this for a short time each day and it will get easier as long as you do it regularly.

It is also useful to get together with another musician and practice this technique between the two of you. E.g. have a guitarist play short phrases and you repeat them. Then swap roles - you improvise short phrases and your friend copies them by ear. This can develop into call and response (question and answer) which is commonly used by Blues musicians and is always entertaining for an audience. Your eventual aim should be to be able to instantly copy any melody and come up with your own variations on it. All great players can do this.

CALL AND RESPONSE

As mentioned previously, **call and response** is a typical Blues technique where one instrument or voice answers another. In the following example, the harmonica does not play in the first two bars. On the recording, the guitar in these two bars and then the harmonica answers in the following two bars. When the example repeats, space has been left for you to play the response. When you are copying a phrase played by a different instrument (in this case guitar) you may have to change some of the expressions to suit the harmonica, but try to imitate the articulations of the original phrase as closely as possible.

 1.0 (CD2)   **Guitar, Then Harmonica**

LEARNING VOCAL MELODIES

You can learn a lot about phrasing by copying vocal melodies. Because singers have to breathe, their phrasing sounds more natural than an instrumentalist who plays endless fast notes. Although this may impress a few of their friends until the novelty wears off, it won't move people the way a great melody does.

Singers have to fit their melodies to lyrics and get the meaning of the song across to the audience. This means choosing the most effective notes and creating the right mood with the melody and phrasing. Since most harmonica players tend to overplay, studying vocal phrasing can lead to a more authentic Blues sound and more emotion and communication in your playing

The best way to learn a vocal melody is to sing it before you play it. Sing the melody using either the song lyrics or any syllables you like. Do this until you have it in your memory. Then find the notes on the harmonica and play the melody in its simplest form until you have it memorized.

The final step is to add some expressive techniques like bends or vibrato. Use these to get as close as possible to the expressions used by the singer. If you are unsure of the expressions, listen carefully to the singer and then imitate the expressions with your voice and then transfer them to the harp in the closest way you can. Singing is the memory link between your ears and the muscles used to produce sounds on your instrument.

The following example demonstrates a vocal phrase which is then played by the harmonica. once you know it, create your own variations. Learn to play the melody of every song you know. This will prepare you better for playing with other musicians and will also help you build a repertoire of your own.

 1.1 Vocal Memorizing Demo - sung then played

One of the most common situations where call and response is used is when you are playing fills in between lines sung by a vocalist. This is demonstrated in the following example. The trick here is learning to play lines that fit well between the vocal lines instead of running over the top of them. First learn to copy the melody of the song and then come up with your own variations, then finally play a response which is different to the melody but complements it - like the singer is asking a question and you are providing the answer. Audiences love call and response and other musicians always like playing with harp players who can do it well.

2. Come Back Darlin'

LEAVING SPACE BETWEEN PHRASES

One of the most effective ways of soloing in Blues is to imagine the harmonica is taking the place of a vocalist and to use a vocal style of phrasing.The following example demonstrates the vocal melody from the previous example played by the harmonica. This time the harmonica leaves a space for another instrument to play the response (in this case a piano). Leaving space between phrases also gives time for the listener to comprehend and enjoy what you just played.

3.0 Harp plays melody, Piano responds

CD 2 3.1 Wailin'

This Blues solo uses most of the techniques you have learnt, and uses a vocal style of phrasing. Listen to the CD to hear the expressions created by the use of each technique. As mentioned earlier, a good way to learn any new solo is to sing along with the recording to help get the sound in your memory. By now you should have a good grasp of the basics of harmonica playing. As well as learning the new sounds and techniques in the book, it is essential to listen to your favourite albums and play along with them, and also to play with other musicians as often as possible. Guitar and harmonica sound particularly good together, as do piano and harmonica. If you are serious about music it may also be worth taking some lessons, particularly in the area of understanding music. The most important thing is to just keep on playing and keep on learning new melodies and then creating your own variations on them. By doing this, you will develop your own style.

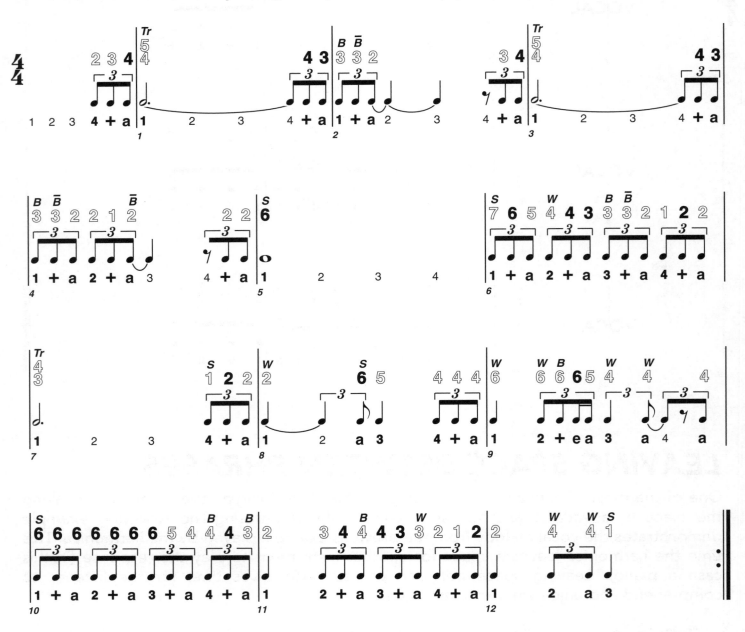

LESSON NINETEEN

EIGHT BAR BLUES

Although the majority of Blues songs follow the 12 bar format, there are many variations. The most common of these is the **eight bar Blues**. The following solo is a typical example. It is based on the progression from the song *Key to the Highway*, which was written by Big Bill Broonzy and made famous by Little Walter.

CD 2 **4.** **Ridin' The Line**

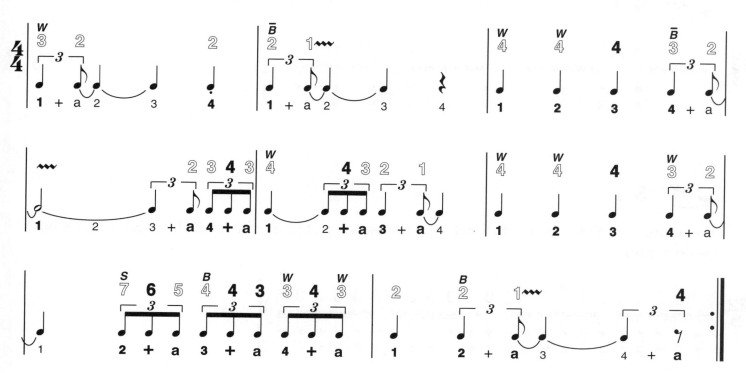

Here is the chord progression this solo is played over. Get a friend to play the chords on guitar or keyboard while you improvise over it. This is a great way to become familiar with any new form, or any song.

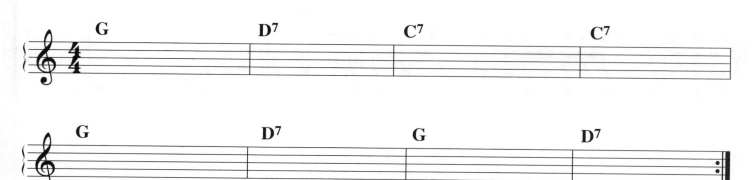

108

THE TWELVE EIGHT TIME SIGNATURE ($\frac{12}{8}$)

 This time signature is called the **twelve eight** time signature. It tells you there are **twelve eighth note beats** in each bar.

A bar of eighth notes in twelve eight time sounds the same as a bar of triplets in four four time. Although there are twelve individual beats which can be counted, twelve eight time is usually still counted in four as demonstrated in the following example.

5.0

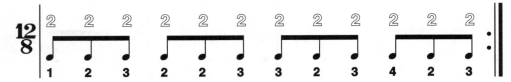

5.1

The beats can also be subdivided into sixteenth notes as shown below. Be careful with the counting.

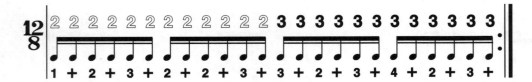

5.2

Here is a Blues lick in $\frac{12}{8}$ time which makes use of sixteenth notes.

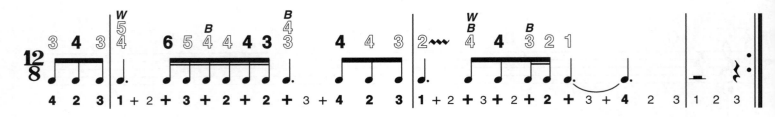

The following solo is written in 12/8 time and is played over another example of an eight bar blues. This one uses the chord progression from a song called *Worried Life Blues* by piano player Big Maceo. It has also been recorded by Otis Spann, and Eric Clapton among others.

6 Coming Home Blues

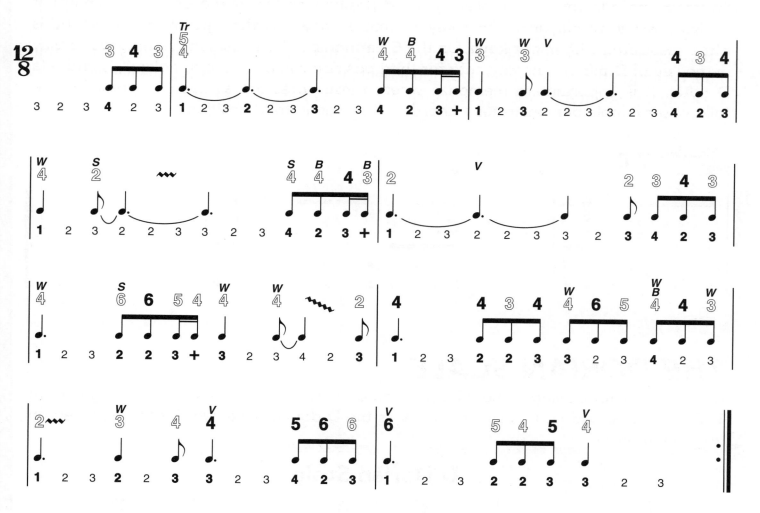

Here is the chord progression underlying the above solo. Notice that it is different from the previous eight bar Blues.

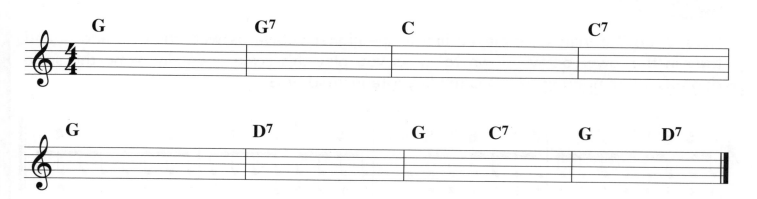

LESSON TWENTY

THIRD POSITION

So far you have learned about playing in first position, and second position (cross harp). It is also possible to play in another key in what is known as **third position**. This sound is often associated with **minor keys**. On the **C harmonica**, third position can be used to play in the key of **D minor**. The key note for third position can be found at holes 1, 4 and 8 (a D note). It is important to memorize where these notes are as soon as possible. The following example demonstrates a chordal riff played in third position.

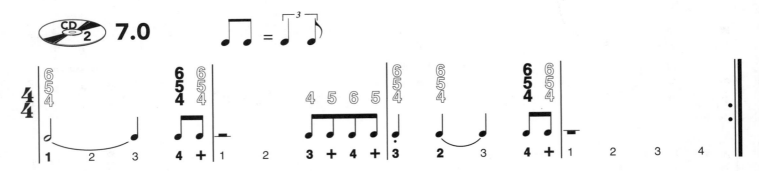

THE DORIAN SCALE

A useful scale for playing in the third position is the Dorian scale or mode. Its degrees are **1**, **2**, **♭3**, **4**, **5**, **6** and **♭7**. It is shown below as the D dorian scale, which can be played on the C harmonica.

D Dorian Scale

D	E	F	G	A	B	C	D
1	**2**	**♭3**	**4**	**5**	**6**	**♭7**	**8**

 7.1

Here is the D dorian scale played first in the higher octave between holes 4 and 8, and then in the lower octave down to 1. As you play this scale, mentally name the scale degrees, remembering that D is the keynote instead of G.

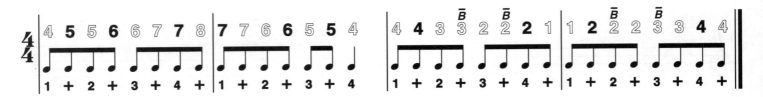

Written below are two traditional songs played in the third position. Both of them are derived from the dorian scale.

 **St James Infirmary**

 Scarborough Fair

SIMPLE AND COMPOUND TIME

Time signatures fall into two basic categories – **simple time** and **compound time**. **Simple time** is any time signature where the basic beat is **divisible by two**. E.g. in $\frac{4}{4}$, $\frac{3}{4}$, and $\frac{2}{4}$ the basic beat is a quarter note which may be divided in half to become two eighth notes per beat. Any time signature where the basic beat is **divisible by three** is called **compound time**. The most common example of compound time is **six eight** time ($\frac{6}{8}$). Other examples of compound time are $\frac{9}{8}$ and $\frac{12}{8}$. In compound time, the basic beat is felt as a dotted quarter note which can be divided by three.

THE SIX EIGHT TIME SIGNATURE

This is the **six eight** time signature.
There are six eighth notes in one bar of $\frac{6}{8}$ time.
The six eighth notes are divided into two groups of three.

10 House of the Rising Sun

This traditional American song is written in $\frac{6}{8}$ time and is played in third position.

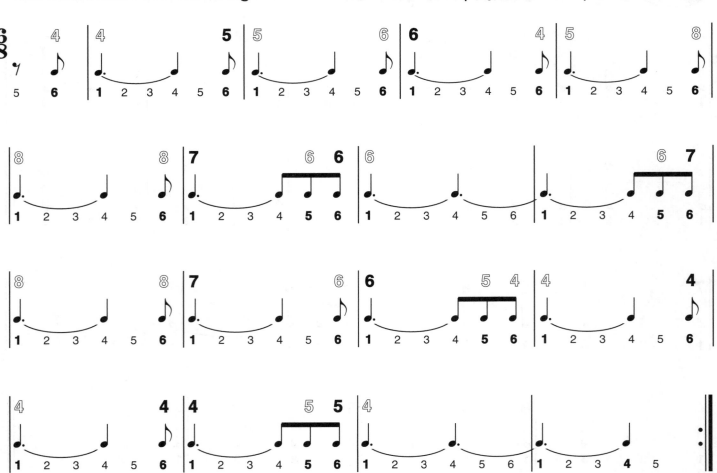

THE BLUES SCALE IN THIRD POSITION

Written below are the notes of the **D** Blues scale which can be played in third position on a C harmonica.

D Blues Scale

D	F	G	A♭	A	C	D
1	♭3	4	♭5	5	♭7	8

 **11.0**

Here is the D Blues scale played over two octaves. As with earlier scales, name the degrees mentally as you play, and try to memorize the scale. This will make things easier when it comes to creating licks from the scale.

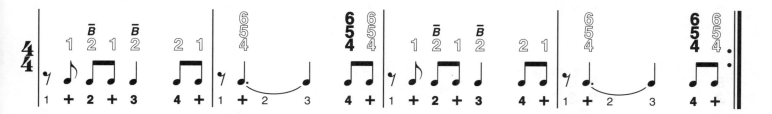 **11.1**

Here is a lick derived from the third position Blues scale.

11.2

This one is a combination of a single note riff and a chord riff played in a call and response style. Try making up some of your own licks from the dorian scale and the Blues scale. The more you do this, the easier it will become.

PLAYING OCTAVES

A technique which is particularly effective when playing in third position is the use of two notes an octave apart (known as "playing octaves"). This involves covering four holes (e.g. **1**, **2**, **3** and **4**) but blocking the middle two (**2** and **3**) with the tongue. This allows only the two outside notes (**1** and **4**) to sound. These notes are an octave apart. This is demonstrated in the following example. Listen to the CD to hear the effect it produces and then try playing along. Space has been left for you to play it by yourself on the repeat.

This technique can take some time to master. Most people can either get three or one notes to sound together at first but not two. Be patient with it and practice it for a short time each day. After a few weeks you will start to gain control of it.

12.0

12.1

Here is a riff using octaves in third position. Once again, space has been left on the recording for you to play it when the example repeats.

Here is a Blues solo using octaves in third position. It is a simplification of the style of Chicago Blues great **Junior Wells**, the all time master of third position playing.

13   Swingin' With Junior

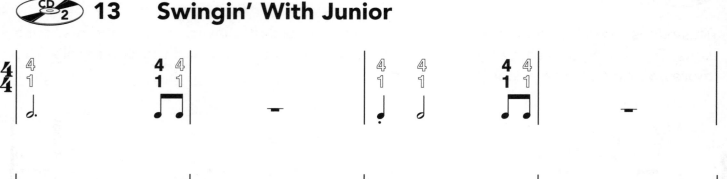

To finish our study of third position playing, here is a solo using ideas from the playing of two great Australian harp players **Ron King** of the Foreday Riders and **"Continental" Robert Susz** of the Mighty Reapers and also Continental Blues Party. Both these players have studied the third position playing of Junior Wells.

14 King Continental

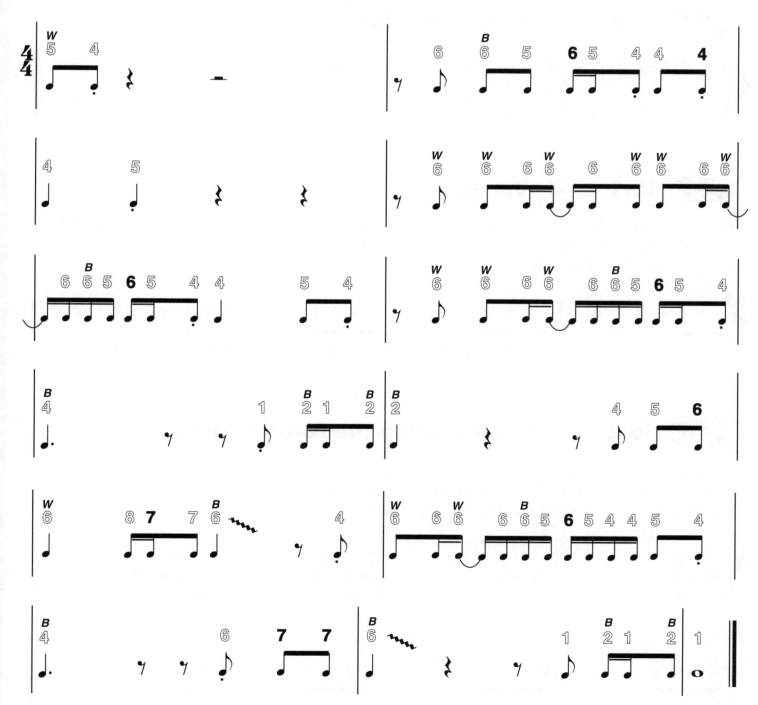

LESSON TWENTY ONE

FOURTH POSITION

As you learnt in the previous lesson, the use of third position enables you to play in **minor keys**. By using **fourth position**, it is possible to play in another minor key. On the **C harmonica**, fourth position can be used to play in the key of **A minor**. The key note for fourth position can be found at holes 6 and 10 (an **A** note). As with any new position, it is important to memorize where these notes are as soon as possible. A good way to begin learning fourth position is to memorize the A natural minor scale, which is shown below.

15.0 Natural Minor Scale

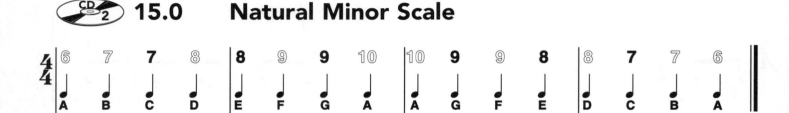

15.1 2 octaves

It is also possible to play a lower octave of this scale by starting with hole 5 as a **bent** note. By using this note, it is possible to play two octaves of the natural minor scale as demonstrated in this example.

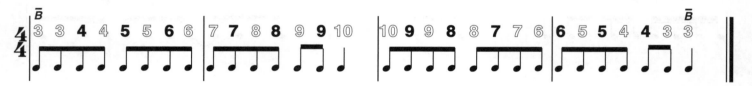

15.2 Sequence Using the Natural Minor

Once you are comfortable with the notes of the scale, try playing some sequences with it, as shown here. It is also recommended that you adapt all of the other sequences you learnt with the C major scale by moving the starting note down from **C** to **A**.

Here are some melodies which are derived from the **natural minor** scale.

 16 God Rest Ye Merry Gentlemen

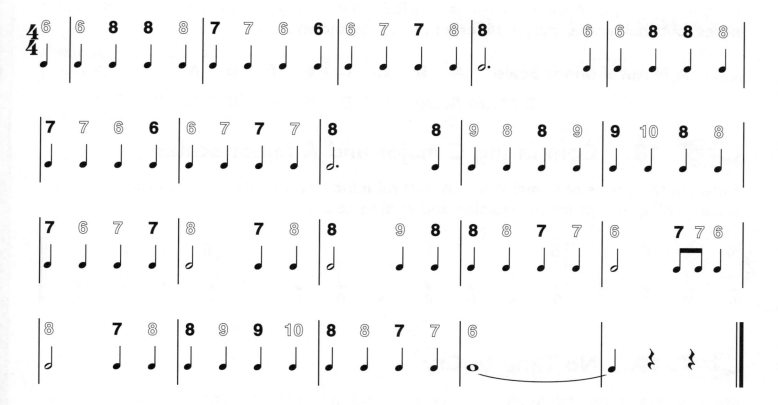

 17 Minor Swing

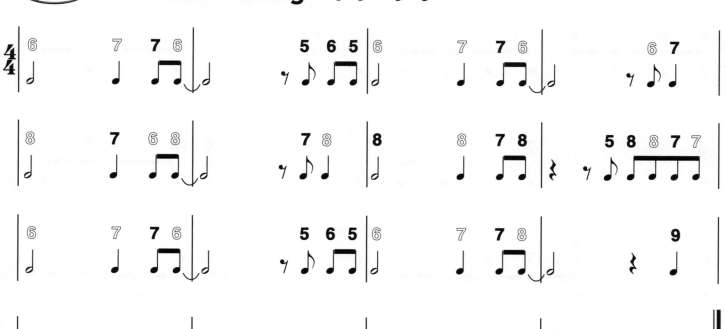

RELATIVE MAJOR AND MINOR KEYS

On any Harmonica, first position and fourth position are closely related. On the C harmonica, first position is used for playing in the key of **C Major**, while fourth position is used for the key of **A minor**. These are called **Relative keys**. Both keys contain the same notes, but their scales start in different places, as shown below.

A Natural Minor Scale   A   B   C   D   E   F   G   A

C Major Scale   C   D   E   F   G   A   B   C

 **18.   Comparing C major and A minor scales**

Here are the scales of **C major** and **A natural minor**. Notice that it is basically the same scale to play, except for the starting and ending notes.

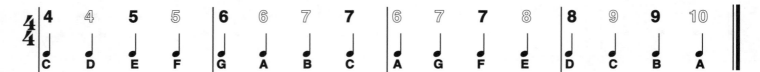

 **19.   No Time to Cry**

Many songs move between a major key and it's relative minor, or vice versa as demonstrated here. The backing to this example has been recorded as a Jam-along track at the end of CD2 (page 178) so you can practice alternating between relative major (1st position) and minor (4th position) keys.

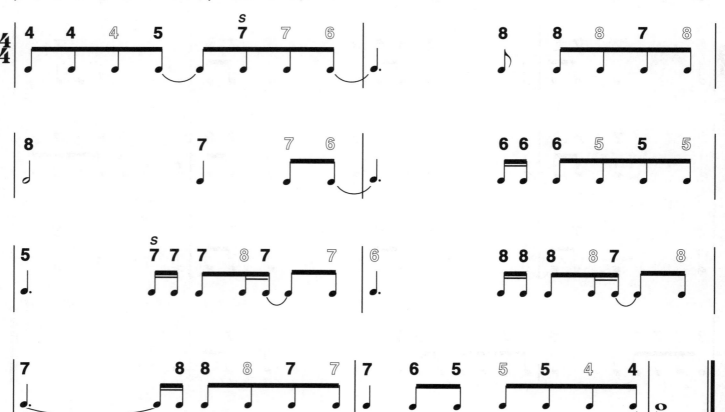

SWINGING SIXTEENTH NOTES

Like eighth notes, it is possible to swing sixteenth notes by playing the first and third notes of the triplet grouping. Swung 16th rhythms are common in Funk, Hip-Hop and Rock which is influenced by these styles. Swing the 16ths in the following example, and then try some of the earlier examples in the book with swung 16ths.

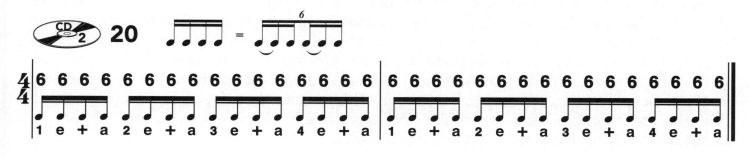

Ma Curly Headed Baby

Here is a melody containing swung 16th notes. This beautiful song was made famous by the great American singer **Paul Robeson**.

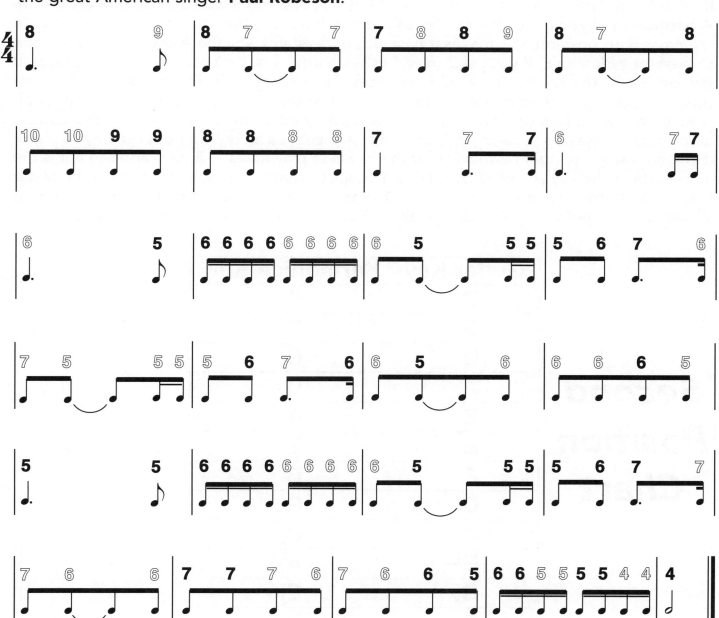

PLAYING IN OTHER KEYS

Everything on the recording accompanying this book uses a **C** harmonica . However, many times when you play with other musicians or play along with your favorite albums, other keys will be used which are not available on a C harmonica. Once you are comfortable playing the C harmonica it is a good idea to get a few others in different keys. The playing techniques are identical regardless of the key you are playing in, only the actual pitch of the notes changes. This means that once you can play a song on the C harmonica, you can transfer it directly to any other harmonica and play the same holes with the same breathing and it will sound just as good. If you are playing an **A harmonica** in first position, you will be playing in the **key of A major**. If you are playing a **D harmonica** in first position, you will be playing in the **key of D major**. This means that if you are playing with a guitarist for example, you can easily find the correct key for many songs simply by choosing the harmonica with that key written on it.

For cross harp playing however, it can sometimes be confusing trying to find the right harmonica to fit with what the other musicians are playing. In this situation it becomes more important to know the sounds on the harmonica as scale degrees. E.g. if a guitarist is playing a **Blues in E** (a common key for Blues), you would use an **A harmonica** to play cross harp in second position. The notes found at holes 2, **3**, **6** and **9** would all be **E notes on the A harmonica**. If you know that the notes at these holes are the first degree of any scale in the cross harp position, this makes it easier to understand why the A harmonica is the one chosen for a Blues in E. If you used any other key harmonica, the notes at these holes would not be E and the harmonica would not work for a Blues in E. There are actually more positions you can use on each harmonica, but these are more advanced and are not dealt with here. The following chart lists all the keys used in music along with the correct harmonica for playing second position cross harp with each key. The easiest way to check if you are using the right harmonica for the key is to play holes 2, **3**, or **6** and see if it is the same note as the key you want by testing it against a guitar or keyboard chord. If the guitar plays a **D chord**, your note should be a **D note**, if the guitar plays an **F chord**, your note should be an **F note**, etc. You can usually tell by ear if you have the correct note or not.

Second Position Chart

Guitar Key	Harmonica Key
C	F
G	C
D	G
A	D
E	A
B	E
F	B
D♭	G♭
A♭	D♭
E♭	A♭
B♭	E♭
F	B♭

When playing in third position, it is more common to play in a minor key. However, third position will also work for a standard Blues which uses seventh chords (e.g. G7, D7, etc.). This means that the guitar key shown in the chart below (e.g. **C**) could be either the key of C or the key of C minor. G could represent the key of G or the key of G minor, etc. To choose the correct harmonica to play in third position, you will need to use a harmonica which is named one whole tone (two semitones) down from the guitar or keyboard key (e.g. for the key of C you would use a B♭ harmonica, for the key of G you would use an F harmonica, etc.). The more you play with other musicians, the easier it gets to pick the right harmonica for the musical situation.

THIRD POSITION CHART

Guitar Key	Harmonica Key
C	B♭
G	F
D	C
A	G
E	D
B	A
F♯	E
D♭	B
A♭	G♭
E♭	D♭
B♭	A♭
F	E♭

CLEANING THE HARMONICA

If you play a harmonica regularly, it will need cleaning after a while to keep the holes and the airways under the reeds clear and in good working order. The best way is to soak the harmonica in a bowl of warm water. Turn the harmonica over and shake it several times while fully submerged to remove any air trapped inside it. Leave the harmonica soaking for about an hour, and then alternately shake it and dip it in the water several more times. Also, use a small implement to clear out any unwanted matter if necessary. The next step is to run the harmonica under a cold tap several times and shake it and then tap it on a semi hard surface to clear the water out. Finally you should try exhaling and inhaling through all of the holes until you are confident they all sound properly. If not, shake and tap the harmonica some more until all of the water comes out.

Harmonicas with a plastic body respond better to cleaning than the wooden bodied type, as the wood will often swell and can cut your mouth when sliding between notes.

When playing in **fourth** position, you are playing in the relative **minor** key of whatever the key of the harmonica is. The chart below shows which key harmonica to use for the minor key of any song. There are exceptions to this, because there is more than one type of minor scale, but this chart will help you pick the correct harmonica most of the time. The other types of minor scales are explained in the section on Chromatic harmonica playing. This is worth looking at and going through with a teacher even if you only intend to play diatonic harmonica. The more you know about how music works, the more musical situations you will feel comfortable playing in.

FOURTH POSITION CHART

Guitar Key	Harmonica Key
A min	C
E min	G
B min	D
F♯ min	A
C♯ min	E
G♯ min	B
D♯ min	F♯
B♭ min	D♭
F min	A♭
C min	E♭
G min	B♭
D min	F

It is worth knowing that the harmonica you choose is the relative major key of the guitar key. Look at the chart below which contains all twelve relative major and minor keys and notice that it corresponds with the fourth position chart shown above. The theory of relative keys, and keys in general is discussed in more detail in the next section of the book, which deals with chromatic harmonica playing. This knowledge is necessary for the chromatic harmonica because it is possible to play in all keys on the one harmonica.

RELATIVE KEYS CHART

MAJOR KEY (I)	C	D♭	D	E♭	E	F	F♯	G♭	G	A♭	A	B♭	B
RELATIVE MINOR KEY (VI)	Am	B♭m	Bm	Cm	C♯m	Dm	D♯m	E♭m	Em	Fm	F♯m	Gm	G♯m

LESSON TWENTY TWO

HARPS IN OTHER KEYS

Once you start playing with other musicians, you will need to get some extra harps in different keys, or else you will be very limited in what you can play along with. The more harps you have, the more keys you can play in. Each key will have a slightly different character. Low notes sound great on low tuned harps such as a G harp, while bends can sound more intense on a higher harp such as a D harp. The most commonly used keys are **A, D, G, C, F** and **B flat**. There are harps tuned in all twelve keys, but these ones will get you through most musical situations.

BENDING EXHALE NOTES

By now you should be getting quite good at bending inhale notes. It is also possible to bend **exhale** notes in the high register of the harmonica (often called "blow note bends"). The most commonly bent exhale notes are holes **7**, **8** and **9**, and sometimes **10**. The technique is similar to the one used when bending inhale notes, except that you are blowing air out through the harmonica.

Exhale bends can be difficult at first but like everything else, they get easier the more you practice them. They are easier to execute on lower sounding harmonicas such as an A harp or a G harp. This is because the reeds are more flexible. The following example demonstrates exhale bends on holes **7**, **8** and **9** using an **A harp** in first position (High octave). Listen to the CD and then practice the example for a short time each day until you can play it with a reasonable amount of control.

22.0   Exhale Bends Using an A Harp

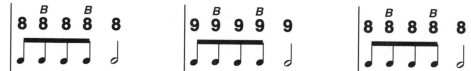

Here is a lick using the exhale bends you have just learnt. It is also played on an **A harp**. Memorize it and then play it along with the recording. Once you start to get some control of blow note bends, get a G harp and practice using them while improvising in first position with the first two Jam-along tracks at the end of CD2 (ex79 and 80).

22.1   Lick Using Exhale Bends

The following solo uses the exhale note bends you learnt on the previous page. It is played on an **A Harp** in first position. It uses ideas from the playing of **Jimmy Reed** and **James Cotton**, two players who are great at using exhale bends in their Blues playing.

On the recording, the whole progression is repeated without the harp so you can play with the band. Play the solo until you have it under control and then try improvising along with the band using exhale bends. Have fun with it!

23. Jimmy James Shuffle

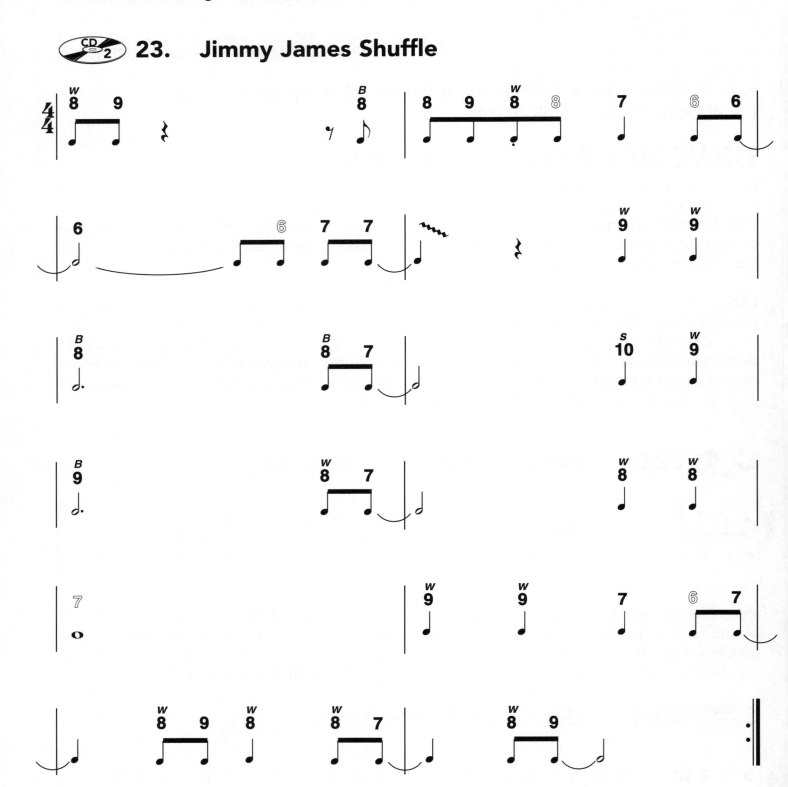

UNDERSTANDING CHORDS

As mentioned in lesson 1, a chord is a group of 3 or more notes played simultaneously. Different types of chords can be formed by using different combinations of notes. The most common type of chord is the **major chord**. All major chords contain three notes, taken from the major scale of the same letter name. These three notes are the 1 (first), 3 (third) and 5 (fifth) degrees of the major scale, so the **chord formula** for the major chord is:

Chord Symbol

1   3   5

The C Major Chord

The C major chord is constructed from the C major scale. Using the above chord formula on the C major scale below, it can be seen that the C major chord contains the notes **C**, **E** and **G**.

C Major Scale

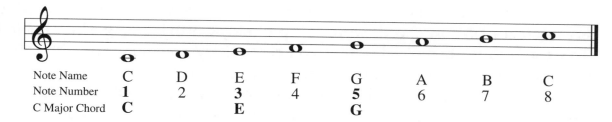

	Note Name	C	D	E	F	G	A	B	C
	Note Number	**1**	2	**3**	4	**5**	6	7	8
	C Major Chord	**C**		**E**		**G**			

Once you have the correct notes for a C chord, you can double each of the notes as many times as you like. As long as the notes are still C, E and G, you still have a C chord. E.g. if you exhale through the harmonica and run your mouth from the bottom to the top of the instrument (holes 1 to 10) you produce a giant C chord covering three octaves, because **all** of the exhale notes on the C harmonica are either C, E or G.

Chords can be played more easily on some instruments than others. Two of the most common instruments used for chord playing are the guitar and the keyboard. Like the harmonica, it is possible to double (or even triple) the notes of a chord on these instruments. As long as you play the correct notes for any chord, they can be arranged in any order, e.g. a C chord could be played C E G, or E G C, or G C E, or even G E C. This is one of the reasons why chords may sound different when played on different instruments.

MELODY AND HARMONY

During the course of this book you have learnt to play songs using both chords and single notes. Any line played in single notes is called a **melody**. Any other accompanying notes such as chords are called **harmony**. There are many ways in which melody and harmony are used in music. One of the most common combinations is to have one instrument play the melody (e.g. harmonica) and another instrument play the harmony (e.g. guitar). When you play a song using chords on the harmonica, usually you are playing a combination of melody and harmony at the same time.

DIFFERENT TYPES OF CHORDS

Apart from starting a chord on the first degree of the scale, it is also possible to build chords on all the other notes of the major scale. A chord built on the second degree of the major scale would contain the 2nd, 4th and 6th notes of the scale. A chord built on the third degree of the scale would contain the 3rd, 5th and 7th notes of the scale, etc. The chord building pattern always consists of the root note (original note), the note two ahead of that note, and the note two ahead of that note, e.g. **C E G**, **D F A**, **E G B**, etc. If you build chords on the first, fourth and fifth degrees of the major scale, you end up with chords I̱, I̱V̱ and V̱ which are the most common chords used for playing the Blues. Because of the pattern of tones and semitones in the major scale, not all the notes in these chords are comparatively the same distances apart. These different distances result in different types of chords such as minor chords and diminished chords. By adding more notes to the chords it is possible to create other chord types such as 7ths, 9ths and 13ths.

It is beyond the scope of this book to deal with all these chord types individually but if you are interested in how chords work, it is probably worth learning a bit of guitar or keyboard. This can also be beneficial in that you can quickly communicate with other musicians by understanding the terms they are using. Another major benefit of learning an instrument like guitar or keyboard is that you can accompany yourself. Many solo Blues and Folk performers use a harmonica rack worn around the neck in order to play guitar and harmonica at the same time. This method is great for your coordination and greatly increases your knowledge of the way notes and chords work together. Apart from this, its a lot of fun and means you are not dependent on other people to make music with. To learn more about chords, chord progressions and keys, see **Progressive Complete Learn to Play Guitar Manual** or **Progressive Complete Learn to Play Keyboards Manual**. For easy reference for playing Blues in any key, here is a chart showing chords I̱, I̱V̱ and V̱ in all keys.

CHORDS I̱, I̱V̱ AND V̱ IN ALL KEYS

KEY	I̱	I̱V̱	V̱	KEY	I̱	I̱V̱	V̱
C	C	F	G	F	F	B♭	C
G	G	C	D	B♭	B♭	E♭	F
D	D	G	A	E♭	E♭	A♭	B♭
A	A	D	E	A♭	A♭	D♭	E♭
E	E	A	B	D♭	D♭	G♭	A♭
B	B	E	F♯	G♭	G♭	C♭	D♭
F♯	F♯	B	C♯				

SECTION 4
Chromatic Harmonica, Understanding Music, Performing in Public

LESSON TWENTY THREE

THE CHROMATIC HARMONICA

The chromatic harmonica is bigger than the diatonic and has a lot more notes available on it. It is possible to play in all keys on the chromatic harmonica by using the **slide**, which is depressed (pushed in) to create extra notes. The most common chromatic harmonica has **12** holes and covers a range of three octaves. Although there are other keys, the **C** chromatic harmonica is the most common and is the one used in this book.

There are two rows of notes on the chromatic harmonica. The top row contains all the natural notes. The bottom row is blocked unless you press in the slide. When you depress the slide, it opens the bottom row which contains all the sharps and flats and at the same time blocks off the top row of notes. The use of the slide gives you **24** holes instead of 12.

HOLDING THE CHROMATIC HARMONICA

The left hand position for holding the chromatic harmonica is identical to that of the diatonic, but there are two possible positions for the right hand. Some players prefer to control the slide with their index finger and use the position in the photo on the left. Others prefer to control the slide with their thumb and use the position in the photo on the right. Experiment with both positions and use whichever is most comfortable.

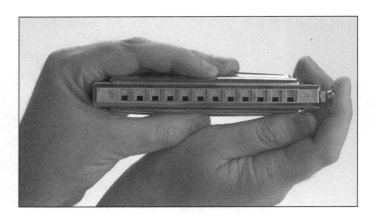 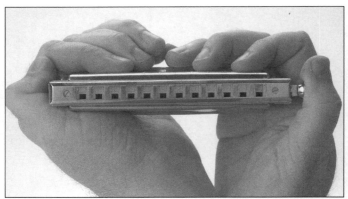

As mentioned above, by using the slide you double the number of notes available on the chromatic harmonica. The following example demonstrates the four notes available from hole number **1**. The first note is an exhale note without the slide depressed (pushed in). This is followed by a different exhale note on hole 1 created by pushing in the slide. This process is then repeated with inhale notes. Listen to the CD and then try it yourself.

 **24.   Using the Slide on hole number 1**

UNDERSTANDING MUSIC

Although it is possible to play the harmonica totally by ear, you can get a lot further by learning to read and understand written music. Since it is the brain which issues the information for playing, it is most important to train the brain to recognise sounds and to build up a bank of knowledge which makes it easier to understand the whole process of making music. This has the added benefit of helping you to relate to what other musicians are playing and understanding the way a song's melody and its accompaniment work together, as well as making it easier to understand the sheet music of any song you wish to learn.

STANDARD MUSIC NOTATION

The musical alphabet consists of **7** letters:

A B C D E F G

Music is written on a **STAFF**, which consists of 5 parallel lines. Notes are written on these lines and in the spaces between them.

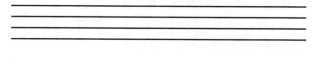

MUSIC STAFF

THE TREBLE or **'G' CLEF** is placed at the beginning of each staff line. This clef indicates the position of the note G.

TREBLE or → **'G' CLEF**

G Note

The **head** of a note indicates its position, on the staff, e.g.:

Notehead

This is a G note

This is an E Note

When the note head is below the middle staff line the stem points upward and when the head is above the middle line the stem points downward. A note placed on the middle line (**B**) can have its stem pointing either up or down.

LEARNING THE NOTES ON THE STAFF

To remember the notes on the lines of the staff, say:
Every **G**ood **B**oy **D**eserves **F**ruit.

The notes in the spaces spell:

F A C E

Extra notes can be added above or below the staff using short lines, called **LEGER LINES**.

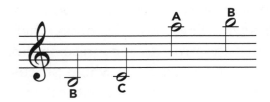

NOTE VALUES

This table shows the most common notes used in music and their respective time values (i.e. length of time held). For each note value there is an equivalent rest, which indicates a period of silence.

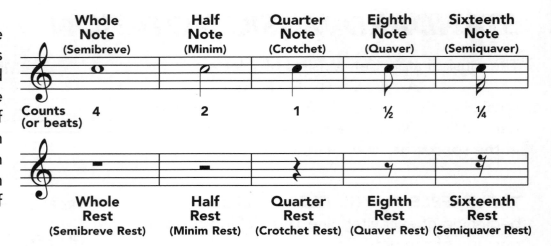

THE NOTE TREE

A useful way to view the relative values of notes and rests is to use a **note tree** (shown below). This makes it easy to see the way notes can be subdivided to create smaller values exactly half the length of the one above it. Although the note tree shown here ends with eighth notes, it is possible to subdivide them further to create sixteenth notes, 32nd notes and even 64th notes.

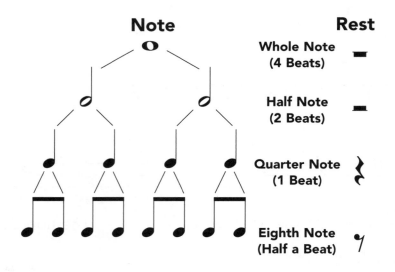

RANGE OF THE CHROMATIC HARMONICA

It is possible to play over a range of three octaves on some chromatic harmonicas, while others cover four octaves. The three octave version is more common and is used for this book. If you have a four octave harmonica, it simply gives you an extra octave of all the notes. The distance of three octaves is shown on the keyboard below. The **lowest note** on the **C chromatic harmonica** is called **middle C**. On a **piano**, this is the C note in the **middle** of the keyboard as shown on the diagram below.

Middle C

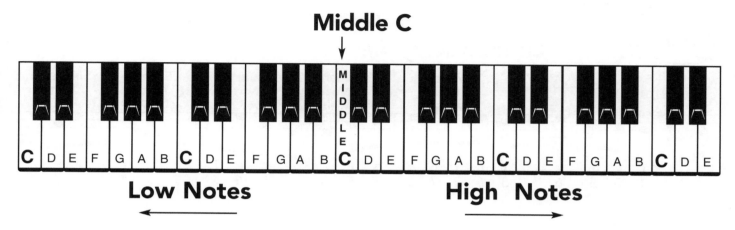

Low Notes   **High Notes**

25.0   C Major Scale Over 3 Octaves

Here is the **C major scale** over **three octaves**. The third (high) octave has the symbol **8va** written above the music. This means it is played an octave higher than written. This symbol is often used for very high notes, as it makes them easier to read. When the notation returns to its normal pitch, the word **loco** is written above the music.

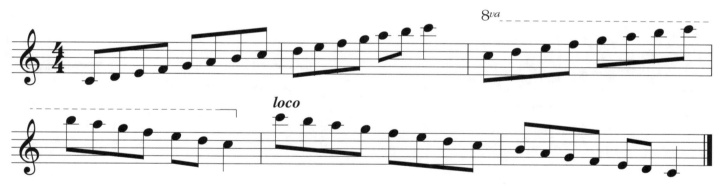

25.1

Playing the major scale on the chromatic harmonica is easy because you don't need to bend any note in any octave. However, the bigger body of the harmonica itself means that the size of the holes and the distance between them is different to that of the diatonic harmonica. Playing **sequences** is a good way of teaching your brain the distances.

PLAYING SONGS ON THE CHROMATIC HARMONICA

Once you have familiarised yourself with the notes on the chromatic harmonica by playing the C major scale and some sequences, the best way to become comfortable with the instrument is to play songs. Over the next few pages you will learn some melodies which Sound great on the chromatic harmonica. The first is the traditional Irish song **Londonderry Air**. All the notes come from the C major scale, and it covers a range of less than two octaves, so it is not difficult to play. Play it slowly and make sure you are producing a strong, even tone.

26   Londonderry Air

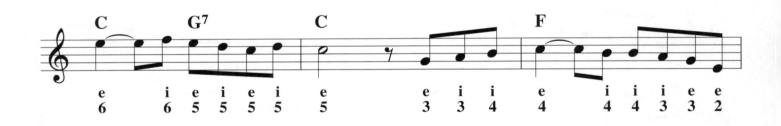

SLURS

A **slur** is a curved line above or below two or more different notes. It indicates that the notes must be played smoothly (called **legato**). To play legato, only tongue the **first** note of the group and keep blowing while you change your mouth positions for the other notes.

CD 2 **27**   **Moreton Bay**

This Australian convict song has a mournful sound and should also be played slowly with a strong, even tone. It is written in $\frac{3}{4}$ time and covers a range of one and a half octaves. This song contains many slurs, which helps create a smooth, flowing sound. Slurs can be used any time for expression even when they are not indicated in the notation.

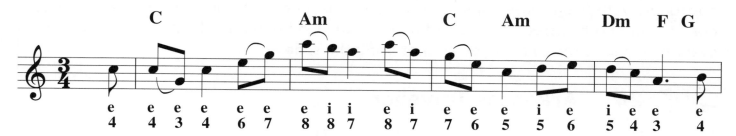

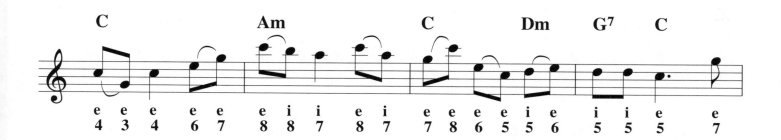

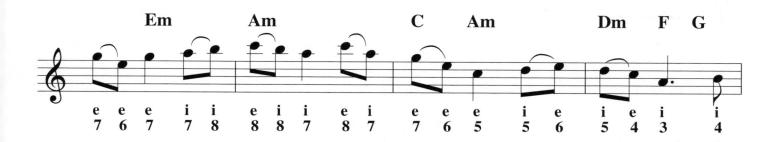

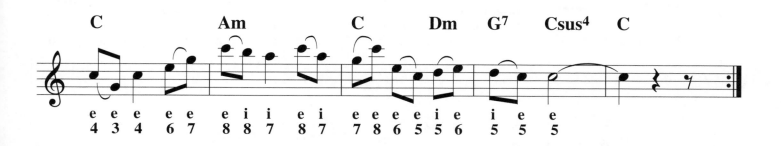

CUT COMMON TIME

The following song features a new time signature which is a variation on the Common time symbol, but this one has a vertical line through it ¢. This is called **cut common time**, or simply cut time. It is also called $\frac{2}{2}$ time and represents two half note beats per bar. In this situation, each half note receives one count. Whole notes receive two counts, while quarter notes receive half a count.

Earlier in the book you learnt to play this song on the Diatonic harmonica in $\frac{2}{4}$ time. There is always more than one way to notate a rhythm. Like $\frac{2}{4}$, Cut common time contains two beats per bar, but because eighth notes are used here instead of sixteenth notes, it is easier to read.

Since you already know how to play this melody on the diatonic harmonica, you should have no trouble with it on the chromatic. It is recommended that you learn as many songs as possible on both types of harp. Although the numbering is slightly different, almost everything else is the same if you are not using the slide.

28 **Arkansas Traveller**

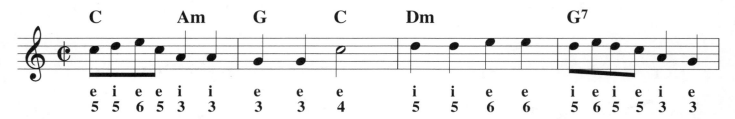

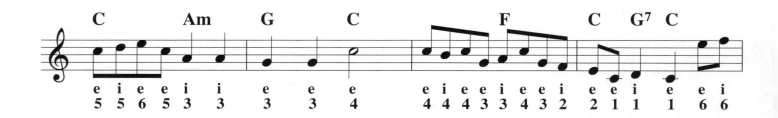

Here are two more melodies to help you become familiar with the layout of the chromatic harmonica. They both sound best when played at a fast tempo, but learn them slowly at first and then gradually increase the tempo once you are comfortable with the notes.

29 The Irish Washerwoman

30 When Johnny Comes Marching Home

This one is in the key of A minor which would be fourth position on a diatonic harp. Since no bending is required on the low notes of a chromatic, it can still be thought of as first position.

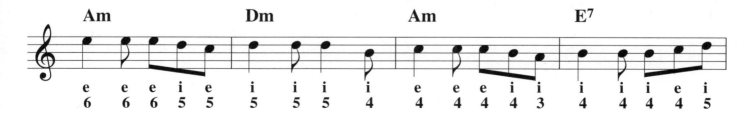

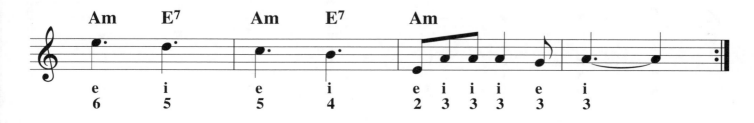

OCTAVES ON THE CHROMATIC HARP

Playing octaves on the chromatic can be difficult at first because the notes are four holes apart instead of three. This means you have to block three holes with your tongue instead of two. The following example is a demonstration of several pairs of octaves on the chromatic harmonica. Practice the technique using exhale and inhale notes in one position before trying the whole exercise. It is difficult so be patient and practice it for a short time each day among your other exercises. Once you can do the basic exercise, try playing some scales in octaves as demonstrated in example 31.1.

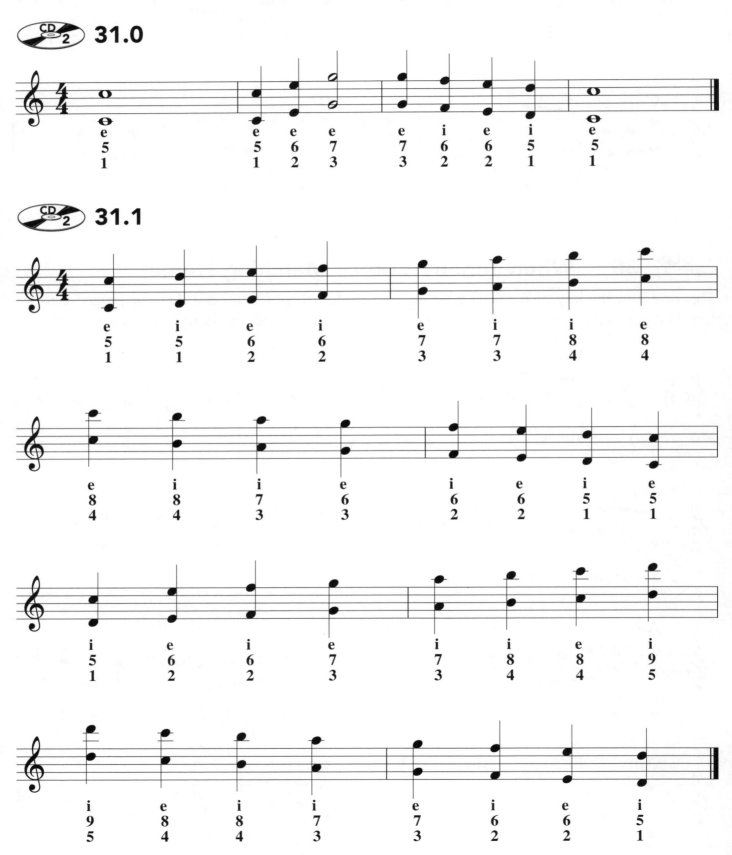

The next step is to play some melodies in octaves as shown here. There are no breathing indications under the notes here, but you already know all the notes so this shouldn't be a problem. If you have trouble, simply listen to the recording and imitate the sounds you hear.

CD 2 **32** **When the Saints go Marchin' in.**

CD 2 **33** **Lonely Hours**

This one is a Blues in third position in the key of D minor. It is similar to one you learnt earlier on the diatonic harp. All the positions are easier to play on the chromatic because there is no bending involved. **Bending notes on the chromatic is not recommended as it can damage the harp!**

DEVELOPING YOUR MUSIC READING

Because it is possible to play in all keys on the chromatic harmonica, it is possible to play a lot of music which could not be played on a diatonic harmonica. Some music can be learned simply by listening to recordings and imitating what you hear. However, recordings only began in the 20th century and there is a whole world of great music written before the 20th century which is unavailable to you if you can't read music.

Even where there are recordings, as music becomes more complex it is harder to learn by ear. If you can read music well, you can often learn a new piece of music in a very short time. This ability allows musicians to play easily with a new group they have never played with before by the use of **"charts"** which contain the melody and chord changes to songs. If you intend to play Jazz or Classical music, it is essential to develop your ability to read and understand music in all keys.

The first step in developing this ability is learning to read scales and simple tunes without the aid of inhale and exhale or hole number markings. Shown below is the notation for a C major scale in quarter notes. You can already play this without even thinking. Play through it watching the notation and say the name of each note to yourself as you play.

34.0

The next step is recognising the notes in different octaves. Here is the C major scale played over two octaves in eighth notes and then sixteenth notes. Don't let the notation for the higher notes scare you. They are simply repeats of the lower notes an octave higher. On the recording the harmonica has been omitted when the example repeats. Play along with the drumbeat while reading the notation. Think the names of the notes as you go. Once you can do this with sixteenth notes, you are well on your way.

34.1

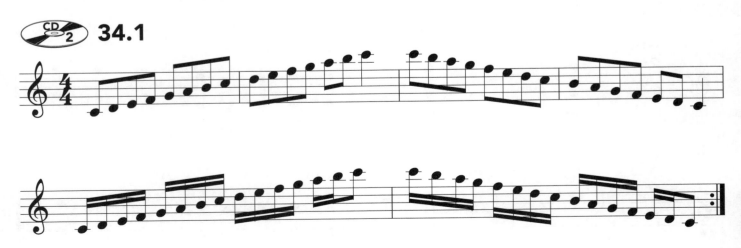

Once you can recognise the notes from the notation, the best way to develop your reading is by doing lots of it! The most enjoyable way to do this is to read melodies. Here are some to practice. Read each one until you can play it from memory and then close your eyes and concentrate on playing with feeling and a beautiful tone.

The following melody is written in Cut Common time. The melodies are only a few examples. It is recommended that you purchase a book of song melodies and start learning the ones in C major. By the end of this book, you will understand how to read melodies in all the other keys as well. It is also a good idea to work your way through method books for other wind instruments, particularly Flute books, as the lowest note on the flute is **middle C** - the same as the lowest note on a C Chromatic harmonica.

37   The Happy Wanderer

LESSON TWENTY FOUR

SOLVING READING PROBLEMS

As you read through these melodies, notice how many different rhythms are used, but the notes remain the same. When you encounter problems in reading music, it is a good idea to practice pitch reading and rhythm reading separately, as most problems are one or the other and by separating them you can zero in on the exact thing you need to work on without any other complications.

Each time you solve a reading problem, you make it easier to solve the next one you encounter because many note sequences and rhythms occur again and again in music.

CD 2 38   **Into the Sun**

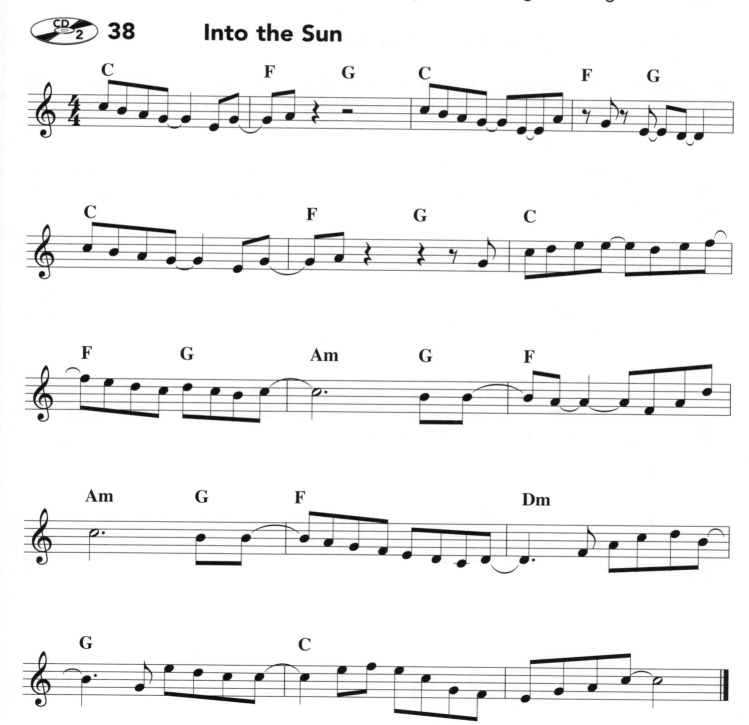

POSITIONS ON THE CHROMATIC HARP

As mentioned earlier, it is possible to play in all positions on the chromatic without bending notes. In fact, attempting to bend notes can damage the reeds and this can be expensive to repair. Once you are comfortable reading melodies in the key of C, the next step is to read some in keys relating to second, third and fourth positions.

You have already learnt the following melody in third position on the diatonic harp, so you will have no trouble playing it on the chromatic. Read the notation and notice that the same notes are used as in C major, but the melody keeps returning to (and ends with) a **D** note rather than a C note. This is because it is in the key of D minor. Minor keys are discussed in more detail in lesson 32. For now, just notice that the sound is different when the same notes are used around a different central point.

39   **St James Infirmary**

As indicated above, the eighth notes in this song are swung. Reading swung eighths is no different in standard notation to the harmonica notation you learnt earlier in the book.

Here is a melody your learnt in fourth position on the diatonic harp earlier in the book (CD2 ex 17). This time it is the third position in the key of D minor.

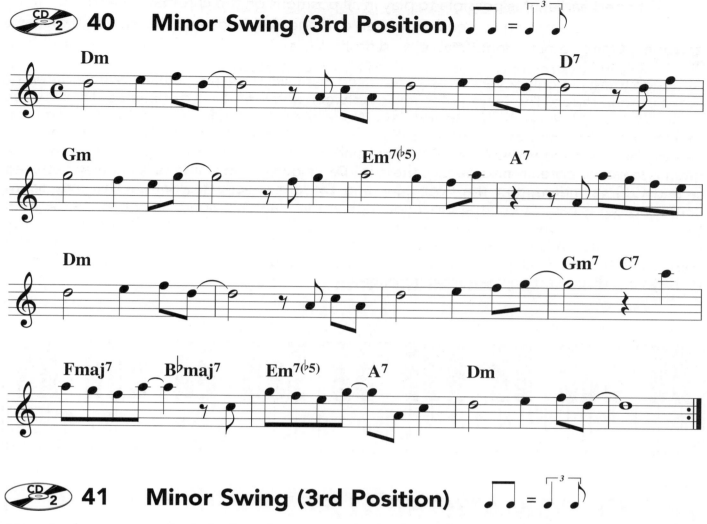

Here is the same melody in fourth position in the key of A minor for chromatic harp. On the recording, space has been left for you to play along with the band.

LESSON TWENTY FIVE

SHARPS (♯) AND FLATS (♭)

Although there are only seven letter names used in music, there are actually **twelve** different notes used in music. The extra notes fall in between some of the letter names. These notes are indicated by the use of **sharps and flats**. A sharp is indicated by the symbol ♯ and means that the pitch is **raised by a semitone**. E.g. the note **C sharp** (**C♯**) is higher than C and falls halfway between the notes C and D. A flat is indicated by the symbol ♭ and means that the pitch is **lowered by a semitone**. E.g. the note **D♭** is lower than D and falls halfway between D and C. This means that the notes **C♯** and **D♭** are exactly the same. This may seem confusing but is easy to understand if you look at the piano keyboard shown in the diagram below. The white notes are all the natural notes (**A B C D E F G**) and the black notes are the sharps and flats. D♯ is the same as E♭, F♯ is the same as G♭, etc. Sometimes one is used and sometimes the other, depending on the musical situation and the **key** the music is written in. Keys are discussed on the following page.

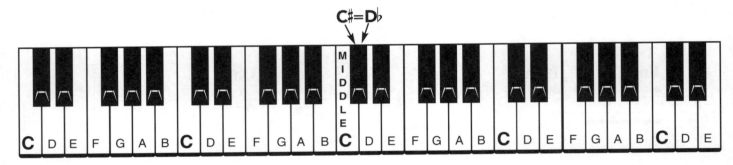

THE CHROMATIC SCALE

As mentioned above, with the inclusion of sharps and flats, there are 12 different notes within one octave. The notes **EF** and **BC** are always one **semitone** apart. All the other natural notes are a **tone** apart. Sharps (♯) and flats (♭) are found between the notes that are a tone apart. If you combine all the natural notes with the sharps and flats found in between them, you end up with what is called the **chromatic scale**. This scale contains all the notes used in music. The chromatic scale is made up of twelve consecutive semitones.

INTERVALS

An **interval** is the distance between any two notes. Intervals are named in numbers which are larger or smaller depending on how many letter names apart the notes are. E.g. C to D is the interval of a second (C=1, D=2), C to E is the interval of a third (C D E = 1 2 3), C to F is the interval of a fourth, etc. There are actually various different types of intervals (major, minor, etc). This is explained in detail in lesson 31. At this stage it is enough to be aware that different notes can be specific distances apart based on their letter names and the number of semitones between them, and that these distances are called intervals. If you wish to pursue music more seriously, it is important to understand and be able to hear all the different intervals. Any good keyboard or theory teacher will be able to help you with this.

USING THE SLIDE

Sharps and flats are played on the chromatic harp by using the slide. When the slide is pushed in, both inhale and exhale notes sound **one semitone higher** than they do without the slide pushed in, thus creating a **sharpened** version of the natural note. In the following example, each time the slide is pushed in, the note has an **S** below it. Follow the notation while listening to the CD and then try playing it. It is important to release the slide as you begin to play the next note. Don't worry if you have trouble with this, the example is simply a demonstration to show you how it works. With practice it gets easier and easier.

CD 2 **42**   **Using the Slide to Play Sharps**

CD 2 **43**   **The Ash Grove**

Sometimes a sharp or flat occurs only once in a piece. In this traditional British folk song, the note **F♯** occurs only in bar 15 . This note is played by inhaling through hole **6** and pushing in the slide. Release the slide just as you begin to breathe out to play the following **G** note.

LESSON TWENTY SIX

MORE ABOUT MAJOR SCALES

The **C major scale** contains the following notes.

$$C \quad D \quad E \ F \quad G \quad A \quad B \ C$$

tone tone semitone tone tone tone semitone
T T ST T T T ST

The distance between each note is a tone except for **EF** and **BC** where the distance is only a semitone. A **semitone** is the smallest distance between two notes used in western music. Shown below is the pattern of tones and semitones in the major scale, with the **scale degrees** written under the notes.

Note	C	D	E	F	G	A	B	C
Scale Degree	1	2	3	4	5	6	7	8
Tone Pattern		T	T	ST	T	T	T	ST

T = Tone
ST = Semitone

MAJOR SCALE PATTERN

Once you know the pattern of tones and semitones used to create the C major scale, you can build a major scale on **any** of the twelve notes used in music. It is important to memorize this pattern, which is shown below.

Tone   Tone   Semitone   Tone   Tone   Tone   Semitone

The **semitones** are always found between the **3rd and 4th**, and **7th and 8th** degrees of the scale. All the other notes are a tone apart.

THE G MAJOR SCALE

To demonstrate how the major scale pattern works starting on any note, here is the **G major scale**. Notice that the 7th degree is F sharp (F♯) instead of F. This is done to maintain the correct pattern of tones and semitones and thus retain the sound of the major scale (**do re mi fa so la ti do**).

$$G \quad A \quad B \ C \quad D \quad E \quad F\sharp \ G$$

tone tone semitone tone tone tone semitone
T T ST T T T ST

Here is the notation for the G major scale. The F♯ note is the same as the one you learnt to play earlier in The Ash Grove (hole 6 inhaled with the slide pushed in).

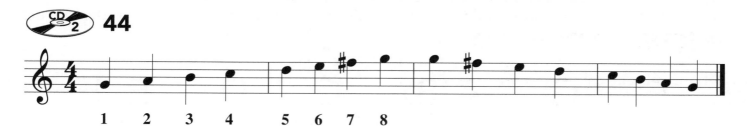

KEY SIGNATURES

As you learnt in lesson 7, when a song consists of notes from a particular scale, it is said to be written in the **key** which has the same name as that scale. For example, if a song contains notes from the **G major scale**, it is said to be in the **key of G major**. Instead of writing a sharp sign before every F♯ note, it is easier to write just one sharp sign after the treble clef. This means that **all** F notes on the staff are played as F♯, even though there is no sharp sign placed before the note. This is called a **Key Signature**. Key signatures are discussed in more detail in lesson 28.

45 **Brahms' Lullaby in the Key of G**

Play all F notes as **F♯** as indicated by the key signature.

Key signature of G Major

THE F MAJOR SCALE

By starting the major scale pattern on the note F, it is possible to create an **F major scale**. In this scale, it is necessary to flatten the 4th degree from B to **B♭** to maintain the correct pattern of tones and semitones.

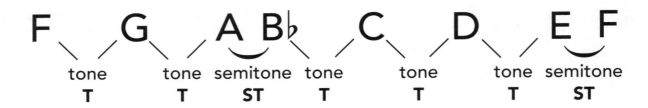

 **46**

Here is the F major scale written in standard notation with the scale degrees written under the notes. The B flat note is played by **inhaling** through the **3rd** hole and pressing in the slide.

 **47**   **All Through the Night**

This melody is derived from the F major scale and is therefore said to be in the **key of F Major**. Play all B notes as **B♭** as indicated by the key signature.

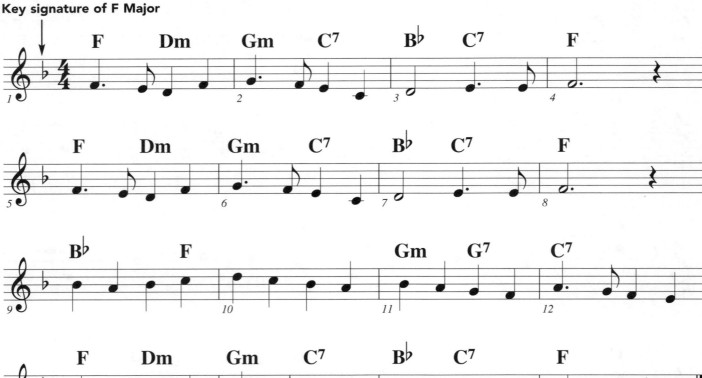

LESSON TWENTY SEVEN

PLAYING THE CHROMATIC SCALE

In the previous examples, the melody consists entirely of notes from the major scale. However, many melodies use notes from outside the major scale, particularly in styles such as Blues, Jazz, Rock and Funk. These "outside notes" relate to the chromatic scale starting on the same note as the major scale of the key the music is written in. Therefore, if you have a piece of music in the key of C which contains notes which are not in the C major scale, you can relate these notes to the **C chromatic scale**.

 **48.0**

This example demonstrates one octave of the C chromatic scale. The notes played with the slide depressed have an **S** under them, with the correct hole number written underneath.

ENHARMONIC NOTES

The "in between" notes in the chromatic scale can be described as either sharps or flats. These are called **enharmonic** notes, which means they are the same pitch (e.g C♯ =D♭ and F♯ =G♭). Here is an example demonstrating the use of enharmonic notes.

 **48.1**

You now know all the different notes used in western music (twelve in all). This includes all the natural notes (**A B C D E F G**), plus **F♯**, **C♯**, **G♯**, **D♯**, and **A♯**. Because each sharp notes has another name as a flat, you also know **G♭, D♭, A♭, E♭,** and **B♭**. If you play all twelve notes in succession, you get the **chromatic scale**. As you know, all of the notes in a chromatic scale are **one semitone** apart. To get to know all possible ways of describing any note in a given key, it is a good idea to call notes all notes which are not natural to the key **sharps when ascending** and **flats when descending**.

Like all scales, you will need to be able to play the chromatic scale across the whole range of the harmonica. The following example demonstrates two octaves of the **C chromatic scale**. Take it slowly at first until you can play it smoothly and easily without hesitation. It is a good idea to make the chromatic scale part of your daily practice, as a good knowledge of this scale makes it easy to quickly transpose any melody, as well as making it easier to learn any new scale or key.

49   C Chromatic Scale

Once you can play the C chromatic scale, you already know all other chromatic scales, e.g. to play the **E chromatic scale**, you simply start on the note **E** and play all possible notes until you arrive at the next E note one octave higher or lower, as demonstrated in the following example which contains two octaves of the E chromatic scale.

50   E Chromatic Scale

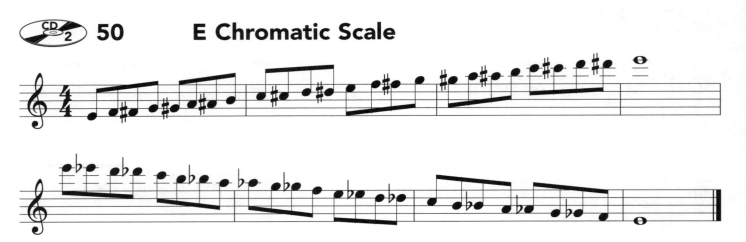

THE NATURAL SIGN

 This is a **natural** sign.

A natural sign cancels the effect of a sharp or flat for the rest of that bar, or until another sharp or flat sign occurs within that bar. Notice the alternation between **F** natural (**F♮**) and **F♯** in example 51.

51.

Now try this 12 bar Blues solo which makes use of **sharp**, **flat** and **natural** signs. It is played in third position in the key of D minor and is derived from the D Blues scale. The only note requiring the use of the slide is **G♯** or **A♭**, which is an **exhale** note on the **3rd** hole with the slide depressed.

52   **Slow and Easy**

LESSON TWENTY EIGHT

MORE ABOUT KEYS AND KEY SIGNATURES

The **key** describes the note around which a piece of music is built. When a song consists of notes from a particular scale, it is said to be written in the **key** which has the same notes as that scale. For example, if a song contains mostly notes from the **C major scale**, it is said to be in the **key of C major**. If a song contains mostly notes from the **F major scale**, it is said to be in the **key of F major**. If a song contains mostly notes from the **G major scale**, it is said to be in the **key of G major**. When playing in any major key other than C, the key will contain at least one sharp or flat, and possibly as many as six. Instead of writing these sharps or flats before each note as they occur, they are usually written at the beginning of the song just before the time signature. These sharps or flats are called a **key signature**. The number of sharps or flats in the key signature depends on the number of sharps or flats in the corresponding major scale. The major scales and key signatures for the keys of **F** and **G** are shown below. Without sharps and flats, these scales would not contain the correct pattern of tones and semitones and would therefore not sound like a major scale.

G Major Scale

Note	G	A	B	C	D	E	F♯	G
Scale Degree	1	2	3	4	5	6	7	8
Tone Pattern		T	T	ST	T	T	T	ST

Key Signature of G Major

The **G major** scale contains one sharp, F♯, therefore the key signature for the key of **G major** contains one sharp, F♯.

F Major Scale

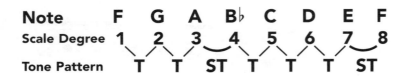

Note	F	G	A	B♭	C	D	E	F
Scale Degree	1	2	3	4	5	6	7	8
Tone Pattern		T	T	ST	T	T	T	ST

Key Signature of F Major

The **F major** scale contains one flat, B♭, therefore the key signature for the key of **F major** contains one flat, B♭.

The reason some scales contain sharps while others contain flats is that there has to be a separate letter name for each note in the scale. E.g. the G major scale contains F♯ instead of G♭ even though these two notes are identical in sound. However, if G♭ was used, the scale would contain two notes with the letter name G and no note with the letter name F. This is the reason for choosing to call the note F♯ in this key. In the key of F major, the note B♭ is chosen instead of A♯ for the same reason. If A♯ was used, the scale would contain two notes with the letter name A and no note with the letter name B. The note each major scale starts on will determine how many sharps or flats are found in each key signature because of the necessity for the scale to have the correct pattern of tones and semitones in order to sound right. The charts on the following page contain the key signatures of all the major scales used in music, along with the number of sharps or flats contained in each key. Because there are 12 notes used in music, this means there are 12 possible starting notes for major scales (including sharps and flats). This means that some of the keys will have sharps or flats in their name, e.g. F♯ major, B♭ major, E♭ major, etc. Keys which contain sharps are called sharp keys and keys which contain flats are called flat keys.

Written below are the key signatures for all the major scales that contain sharps.

The sharp key signatures are summarised in the table below.

Key	Number of Sharps	Sharp Notes
G	1	F♯
D	2	F♯, C♯
A	3	F♯, C♯, G♯
E	4	F♯, C♯, G♯, D♯
B	5	F♯, C♯, G♯, D♯, A♯
F♯	6	F♯, C♯, G♯, D♯, A♯, E♯

*The new sharp **key** is a fifth interval higher*

*The new sharp **note** is a fifth interval higher*

Written below are the key signatures for all the major scales that contain flats.

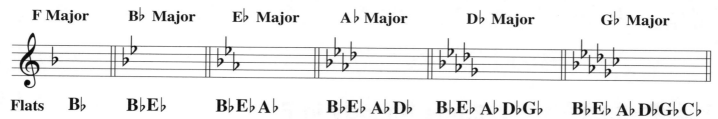

The flat key signatures are summarised in the table below.

Key	Number of Flats	Flat Notes
F	1	B♭
B♭	2	B♭, E♭
E♭	3	B♭, E♭, A♭
A♭	4	B♭, E♭, A♭, D♭
D♭	5	B♭, E♭, A♭, D♭, G♭
G♭	6	B♭, E♭, A♭, D♭, G♭, C♭

*The new flat **key** is a fourth interval higher*

*The new flat **note** is a fourth interval higher*

* Intervals are dealt with in detail in lesson 31.

LESSON TWENTY NINE

TRANSPOSING

Transposing (or transposition) means changing the key of a piece of music. This can apply to a scale, a phrase, a short melody, or an entire song. The ability to transpose is an essential skill for all musicians to develop. The easiest way to transpose is to write the **scale degrees** under the original melody and then work out which notes correspond to those scale degrees in the key you want to transpose to. You should work towards being able to do this in your head instantly, without the need for notated scale degrees. Written below is a short melody played in the key of **C** and then transposed to the keys of **F** and **G**. Play through them and notice that the melody sounds the same, but the overall pitch may be higher or lower. Transpose this melody to all other major keys. You should also try this same technique with other tunes you know. The more you do this, the easier it gets, and the better you are at transposing, the easier it will be to play Jazz.

CD2 53.0   **Melody in C**

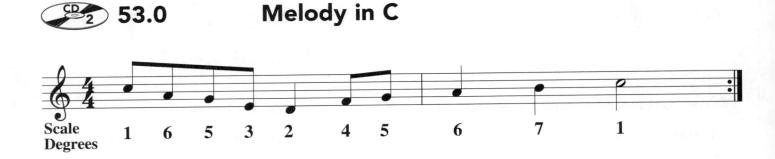

CD2 53.1   **Same Melody in F**

CD2 53.1   **Same Melody in G**

THE KEY CYCLE

There are many reasons why you need to be able to play equally well in every key. Bands often have to play in keys that suit their singer. That could be **F#** or **Db** for example. Keyboard players tend to like the keys of **C**, **F** and **G**, while **E** and **A** are fairly common keys for guitar. Horn players like flat keys such as **F**, **Bb** and **Eb**. Apart from this, Jazz tunes often contain many key changes in themselves. For these reasons, you need to learn how keys relate to each other so you can move quickly between them.

One way to do this is to use the **key cycle** (also called the **cycle of 5ths** or **cycle of 4ths**). It contains the names of all the keys and is fairly easy to memorize.

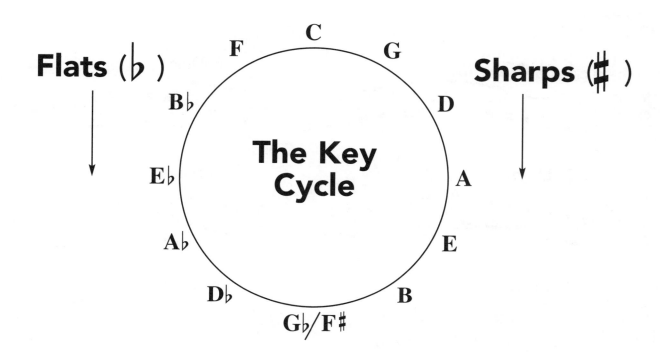

Think of the key cycle like a clock. Just as there are 12 points on the clock, there are also 12 keys. **C** is at the top and contains no sharps or flats. Moving around clockwise you will find the next key is **G**, which contains one sharp (**F#**). The next key is **D**, which contains two sharps (**F#** and **C#**). Progressing further through the sharp keys each key contains an extra sharp, with the new sharp being the 7th note of the new key, and the others being any which were contained in the previous key. Therefore the key of **A** would automatically contain **F#** and **C#** which were in the key of **D**, plus **G#** which is the 7th note of the **A** major scale. When you get to **F#** (at 6 o'clock), the new sharp is called **E#** which is enharmonically the same as **F**. Remember that **enharmonic** means two different ways of writing the same note. Another example of enharmonic spelling would be **F#** and **Gb**. This means that **Gb** could become the name of the key of **F#**. The key of **F#** contains six sharps, while the key of **Gb** contains six flats—all of which are exactly the same notes.

If you start at **C** again at the top of the cycle and go anti-clockwise you will progress through the flat keys. The key of **F** contains one flat (**Bb**), which then becomes the name of the next key around the cycle. In flat keys, the new flat is always the 4th degree of the new key. Continuing around the cycle, the key of **Bb** contains two flats (**Bb** and **Eb**) and so on. **Practice playing all the notes around the cycle both clockwise and anticlockwise**. Once you can do this, play a **major scale** starting on each note of the cycle. In Jazz, there is a lot of movement around the cycle, so the more familiar you are with it, the better.

MAJOR SCALES IN ALL KEYS

The following example demonstrates one octave of the major scale ascending and descending in every key. This will take some to learn but is essential for anyone wanting to play Jazz or Classical music. Learning scales may not seem as interesting as playing melodies, but a little effort at this stage will pay off very well later on, regardless of the style of music you are playing. Memorize the notes of each scale and then try playing it with your eyes closed while visualizing how the notation for the scale would look. Once you have learnt all the scales, you will be able to read music better, play melodies confidently in any key and be able to improvise in any key much more easily.

54.

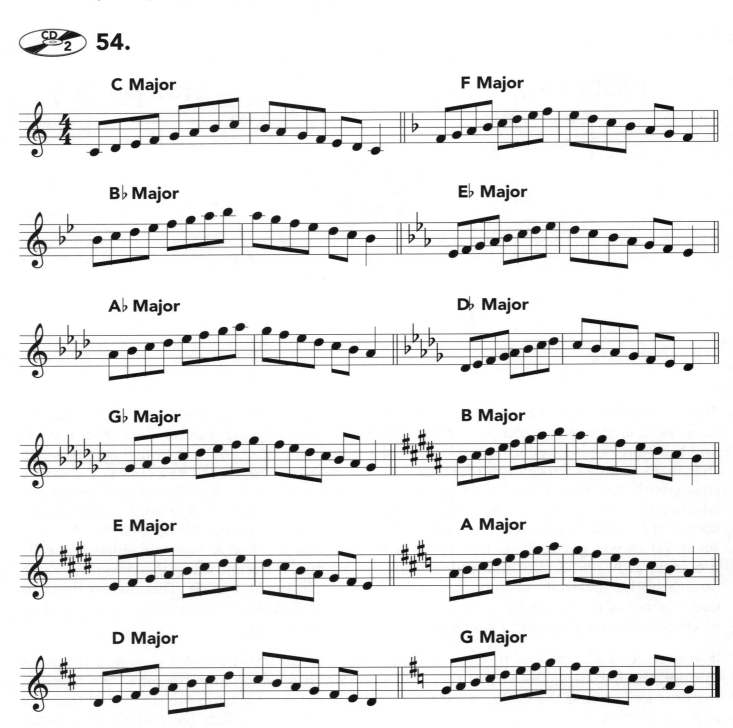

USING THE KEY CYCLE

A good way to become more confident playing in all keys is to take a phrase and play it in every key in order of sharps and flats around the key cycle as shown in the following example which moves around the cycle anticlockwise (adding a new flat for each new key and then continuing through the sharp keys). It is also important to repeat the process going clockwise around the cycle. Write the scale degrees under the notes at first if necessary, and sing them to yourself as you play. If you hope to play Jazz, this ability is essential, as the majority of Jazz tunes modulate around the key cycle in this manner. Make this process part of your everyday practice. The eventual aim is to be able to pick up your instrument and be able to play any melody in any key instantly.

LESSON THIRTY

MORE ABOUT BLUES SCALES

Like the major scale, it is important to be comfortable with the Blues scale in every key. The following example demonstrates the Blues scale moving **up chromatically** through all the keys. Once again, memorise each one and then connect them together until you can play the whole example smoothly and evenly without looking at the notation. Then try reversing the order of the keys (moving down chromatically).

56.   Blues Scales in all Keys

Once you are comfortable with the scales themselves, try inventing a short riff from the Blues scale in one key and then playing the riff in all keys as shown in the following example. If you have trouble with this, memorise all the scale degrees of the riff before transposing it. The riff shown here begins on the flattened 7th degree of the key.

CD 2 57.   Blues Scale Phrase in all Keys

THE KEY OF E♭ MINOR

By keeping the slide **permanently depressed**, it is possible to play third position in the key of **E♭ minor** in a similar manner to third position in the key of **D minor**. You can test this by pressing in the slide and playing any melody you already know in third position (e.g. St James Infirmary). To play the **E** Blues scale, you only need to release the slide for one note (**A** natural - the flattened fifth degree). The following example demonstrates two octaves of the **E♭** Blues scale.

58. Blues Scale in E Flat

59 Falling Down Blues

Here is a Blues solo derived from the **E♭** Blues scale. Notice the use of octaves here.

LESSON THIRTY ONE

INTERVALS

An interval is the distance between two musical notes. Intervals are measured in numbers, and are calculated by counting the number of letter names (**A B C D E F G A**) between and including the notes being measured. Within an octave, intervals are: **Unison** (two notes of the same pitch played or sung together or consecutively), **2nd**, **3rd**, **4th**, **5th**, **6th**, **7th** and **Octave** (two notes an octave apart). Thus **A** to **B** is a **2nd** interval, as is B to C, C to D etc. **A** to **C** is a **3rd** interval, **A** to **D** is a **4th**, **A** to **E** is a **5th**, **A** to **F** is a **6th**, **A** to **G** is a **7th** and **A** to the next **A** is an **octave**.

Intervals may be **melodic** (two notes played consecutively) or **harmonic** (two notes played at the same time). Hence two people singing at the same time are said to be singing in harmony.

INTERVAL QUALITIES

Different intervals have different qualities, as shown below:

Quality	Can be applied to
Perfect	Unisons, 4ths, 5ths and Octaves
Major	2nds, 3rds, 6ths and 7ths
Minor	2nds, 3rds, 6ths and 7ths
Augmented	All intervals
Diminished	All intervals

These intervals can be best explained with the aid of a chromatic scale. If you look at the one below, it is easy to see that since intervals are measured in semitones, they may begin or end on a sharp or flat rather than a natural note.

$$A \quad \frac{A\#}{B\flat} \quad B \quad C \quad \frac{C\#}{D\flat} \quad D \quad \frac{D\#}{E\flat} \quad E \quad F \quad \frac{F\#}{G\flat} \quad G \quad \frac{G\#}{A\flat} \quad A$$

Perfect intervals are **4ths**, **5ths** and **octaves**. If you **widen** a perfect interval by a semitone it becomes **augmented** (added to). E.g. if you add a semitone to the perfect 4th interval **C** to **F**, it becomes the **augmented 4th interval C** to **F#**. Notice that the letter name remains the same—it is not referred to as C to G♭.

If you narrow a perfect interval by a semitone they become **diminished** (lessened). E.g. if you lessen the perfect 5th interval **D** to **A** by a semitone, it becomes the **diminished 5th interval D to A♭**. Again, the letter name remains the same—it is not referred to as D to G#.

Major intervals (2nds, 3rds, 6ths and 7ths) become minor if narrowed by a semitone and **minor** intervals become major if widened by a semitone. A **diminished** interval can be created by narrowing a perfect or minor interval by a semitone. An **augmented** interval can be created by widening a perfect or major interval by a semitone.

INTERVAL DISTANCES

In summary, here is a list of the distances of all common intervals up to an octave measured in semitones. Each new interval is one semitone wider apart than the previous one. Notice that the interval of an octave is exactly twelve semitones. This is because there are twelve different notes in the chromatic scale. Notice also that the interval which has a distance of six semitones can be called either an augmented 4th or a diminished 5th. This interval is also often called a **tritone** (6 semitones = 3 tones).

Minor 2nd - One semitone

Major 2nd - Two semitones

Minor 3rd - Three semitones

Major 3rd - Four semitones

Perfect 4th - Five semitones

Augmented 4th or Diminished 5th - Six semitones

Perfect 5th - Seven semitones

Minor 6th - Eight semitones

Major 6th - Nine semitones

Minor 7th - Ten semitones

Major 7th - Eleven semitones

Perfect Octave - Twelve semitones

The following example demonstrates all of the common intervals ascending within one octave starting and ending on the note C.

60 All Intervals up to an Octave

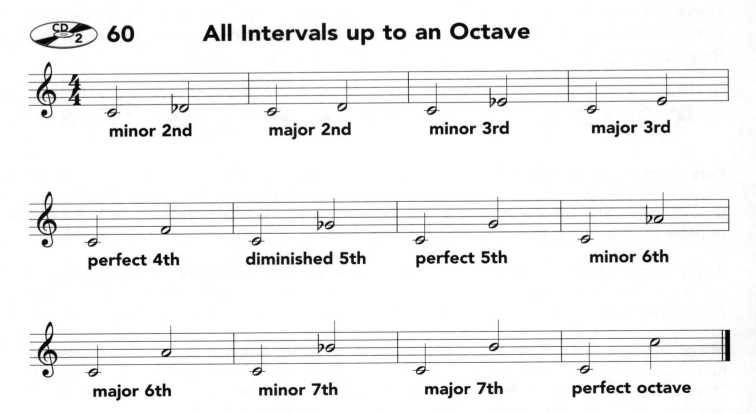

IDENTIFYING INTERVALS BY EAR

Since **all melodies are made up of a series of intervals**, it is essential to learn to identify intervals by ear and be able to reproduce them at will both with your voice and on your instrument. If you can sing something accurately, it means you are hearing it accurately. Here are some ways of developing your ability to identify and reproduce intervals. The example given in the first two exercises is a minor 3rd, but it is essential to go through these processes with **all** intervals.

1. Choose an interval you wish to work on (e.g. minor 3rds). Play a starting note (e.g. C) and sing it. Then sing a minor 3rd up from that note (E♭). Hold the note in your mind while you test its accuracy on your instrument. Then choose another starting note and repeat the process. Keep doing this until you are accurate every time. The next step is to sing the interval (in this case a minor 3rd) downwards from your starting note. Again, do this repeatedly until you are accurate every time.

2. Sing the same interval consecutively upwards and then downwards several times. E.g. start on C and sing a minor 3rd up from it (E♭). Then sing a minor 3rd up from E♭ (G♭). Then another minor third up from G♭ (B♭♭ - which is enharmonically the same as A). Then up another minor 3rd (C an octave higher than the starting note). Once you can do this, reverse the process (Start on C and sing a minor 3rd down to A, then another minor 3rd down and then another, etc).

3. Play and sing a starting note (e.g. C) and then think of it as the first degree of the chromatic scale - sing "one". Now sing the flattened second degree of the scale - sing "flat two". This note is a minor 2nd up from your C note (a D♭ note). Then sing the C again ("one"). Then sing the second degree of the scale (a D note - sing "two"). Next, sing your C Note again ("one"). Continue in this manner all the way up the chromatic scale until you reach C an octave above. The entire sequence goes: 1, ♭2, 1, 2, 1, ♭3, 1, 3, 1, 4, 1, ♭5, 1, 5, 1, ♭6, 1, 6, 1, ♭7, 1, 7, 1, 8, 1. As with the previous exercises, once you can do this accurately (check your pitches on your instrument), reverse the process and sing downwards from the top of the scale, working your way down the chromatic scale again. The downward sequence goes 1(8), 7, 1, ♭7, 1, 6, 1, ♭6, 1, 5, 1,♭ 5, 1, 4, 1, 3, 1, ♭3, 1, 2, 1, ♭2, 1, 1, 1(8).

4. As well as hearing intervals melodically (one note at a time), it is important to be able to hear them harmonically (two notes played together). A good way to develop this is to have a friend play random harmonic intervals on either guitar or keyboard while you identify them. Keep your back to the instrument while you do this, so that you cannot identify the intervals by sight.

It is important to work at these things regularly until they become easy. Don't get frustrated if you can't hear intervals accurately at first. Most people have trouble with this. If you work at it for several months, you will see a dramatic improvement in your musical hearing, and will be able to improvise much more freely as well as being able to work out parts off CDs more easily.

Here are some exercises to help you get more comfortable playing in any key. **Remember to play each one in all possible positions on the fretboard**. Each one is written in a different key, but they are intended to be played in all keys. The first one is a sequence in the key of **D major**.

61.0

61.1

This one alternates between the note **B** and every other note in the **B major scale**, both ascending and descending.

61.2

Don't forget to practice the **chromatic scale** in every key. Here it is in the key of **G♭**.

61.3

Finally, here is one which alternates between the note **A** and every other note in the **A chromatic scale**, once again ascending and descending.

The following example demonstrates a melody in the key of **C** which contains notes from outside the major scale.

62.0   **Key of C**

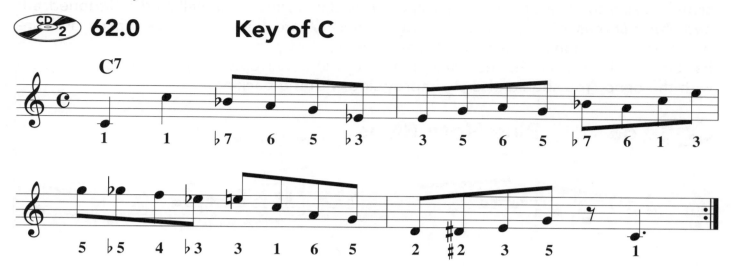

The following examples demonstrate the same melody transposed to the keys of **F** and **G**. Once again, you should transpose it to all the other keys. Before doing this it is worth learning to play the chromatic scale starting on any note. If you do this, it will be easier to play melodies in any key and also make it easier to transpose any melody that you learn in any key.

62.1   **Key of F**

62.2   **Key of G**

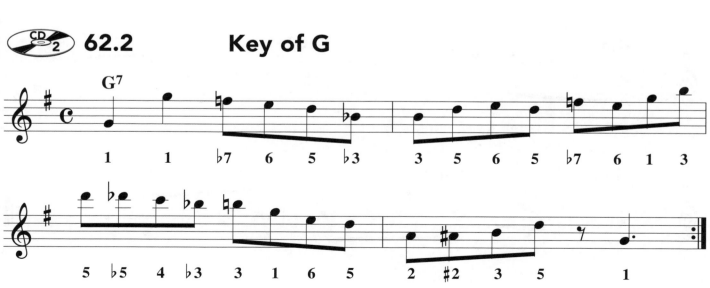

Here is a **Jazz Blues** solo in the key of **F** which makes use of many different intervals. Go through it and analyze the intervals and also the scale degrees against the **F chromatic scale**. Notice the use of both major and minor 3rd degrees, as well as the flattened 5th and 7th degrees of the scale. The ♭3, ♭5 and ♭7 are known as **blue notes** and are particularly common in all forms of Blues. As with many previous examples, the harmonica has been omitted from the recording on the repeat to leave space for you to play the solo with the band. You should also try improvising with the backing.

63 **Blue Note Blues**

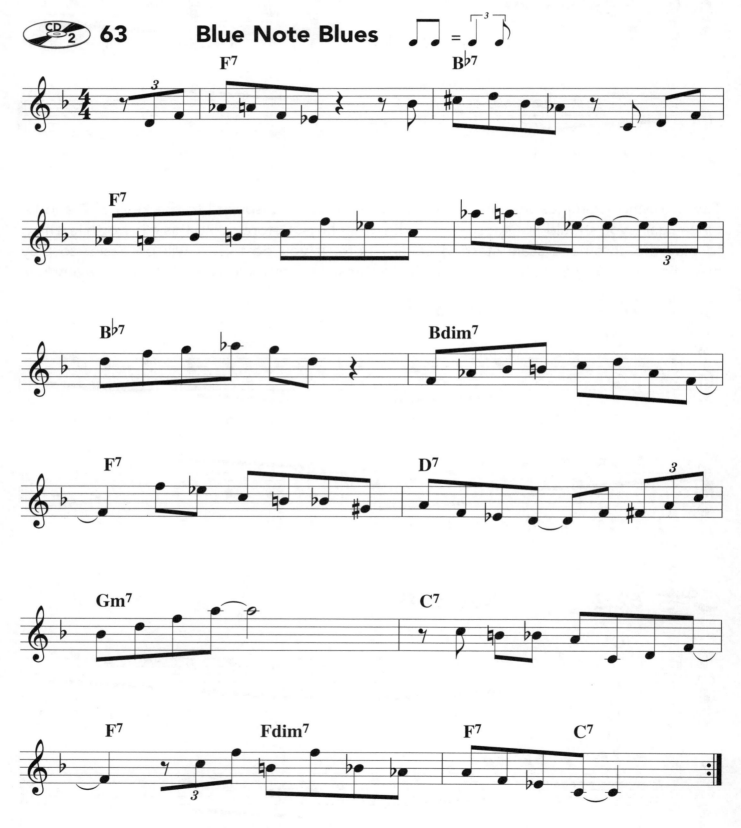

Here is a famous Ragtime melody written by **Scott Joplin**. Originally written for piano, it also sounds great on chromatic harmonica. It is well worth looking for other pieces originally written for other instruments and learning to play them on the chromatic.

CD 2 64 The Entertainer

LESSON THIRTY TWO

MINOR KEYS AND SCALES

Apart from major keys, the other basic tonality used in traditional western music is a **minor key**. Songs in a minor key use notes taken from a minor scale. There are three basic types of minor scale — the **natural minor scale**, the **harmonic minor scale** and the **melodic minor scale**. Written below is the **A natural minor** scale. The degrees of the scale as they would relate to the major scale are written under the note names.

65 A Natural Minor

The A natural minor contains exactly the same notes as the C major scale. The difference is that it starts and finishes on an **A** note instead of a C note. The A note then becomes the key note. Memorize both the scale degrees and the pattern of tones and semitones which make up the scale, then play it with your eyes closed, mentally naming the degrees as you play.

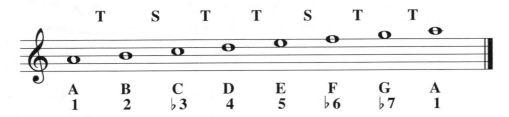

66   The Gypsy's Tale

Here is a melody in the **key of A minor** which is derived from the **A natural minor scale**. Learn it and then try making up your own melodies based on the ideas presented here.

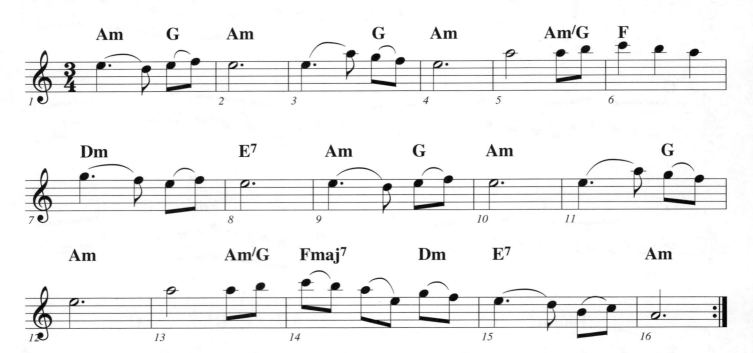

THE HARMONIC MINOR SCALE

The harmonic minor scale has a distance of 1½ tones between the **6th** and **7th** degrees. The raised 7th degree is the only difference between the harmonic minor and the natural minor. This scale is often described as having an "Eastern" sound.

67   **A Harmonic Minor**

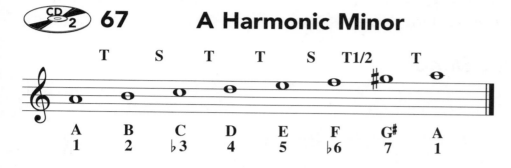

68   **Hahvah Nageelah**

This famous melody is derived from the notes of the harmonic minor scale. It also features the **fermata** or pause sign ⌢ , which is used to indicate that a note or chord is held at the player's own discretion.

THE MELODIC MINOR SCALE

In the **A melodic minor** scale the **6th** and **7th** notes are sharpened when ascending and returned to natural when descending. This is the way the melodic minor is used in Classical music. However, in Jazz and other more modern styles, the melodic minor descends the same way it ascends. An easy way to think of the ascending melodic minor is as a major scale with a flattened third degree.

 69 A Melodic Minor

Melodies in minor keys often contain notes from more than one type of minor scale. The song Greensleeves is mostly derived from the melodic minor, but also contains a flattened 7th degree which comes from the natural minor.

70   Greensleeves

LESSON THIRTY THREE

RELATIVE KEYS

if you compare the **A natural minor** scale with the **C major** scale you will notice that they contain the same notes (except starting on a different note). Because of this, these two scales are referred to as "relatives"; **A minor** is the relative minor of **C major** and vice versa.

Major Scale: C Major

Relative Minor Scale: A Natural Minor

The harmonic and melodic minor scale variations are also relatives of the same major scale, e.g. **A harmonic** and **A melodic minor** are relatives of **C major**.

For every major scale (and ever major chord) there is a relative minor scale which is based upon the **6th note** of the major scale. This is outlined in the table below.

MAJOR KEY (I)	C	D♭	D	E♭	E	F	F♯	G♭	G	A♭	A	B♭	B
RELATIVE MINOR KEY (VI)	Am	B♭m	Bm	Cm	C♯m	Dm	D♯m	E♭m	Em	Fm	F♯m	Gm	G♯m

Both the major and the relative minor share the same key signature, as illustrated below.

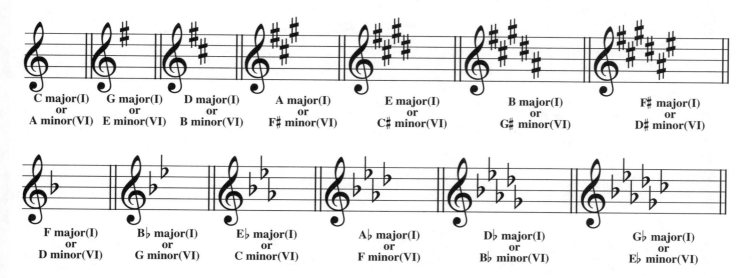

To determine whether a song is in a major key or the relative minor key, look at the last note or chord of the song. Songs often finish on the root note or the root chord. E.g., if the key signature contained one sharp, and the last chord of the song was **Em**, the key would probably be **E minor**, not **G major**. Minor key signatures are always based on the natural minor scale. The sharpened 6th and 7th degrees from the harmonic and melodic minor scales are not indicated in the key signature. This usually means there are accidentals (temporary sharps, flats or naturals) in melodies created from these scales.

Here is a popular South American folk song which moves between the keys of **A minor** and **C major** which are relative keys. This melody makes use of both the harmonic minor and the natural minor. Notice the *rit* symbol at the end indicating a gradual slowing down of the tempo.

When playing traditional melodies, many young players think "oh this is easy and boring, I'd rather be improvising". However, a simple melody played expressively with conviction and a good tone can move people a lot more than a fast nonsensical solo. It is easy to cover up musical inadequacies with a lot of fast notes. Listen carefully to the sound you are making as you play the melody and notice any weaknesses in tone, intonation, expression or rhythm which you may need to work on.

71   **El Condor Pasa**

Here is a piece which alternates between the key of **D minor** and its relative – **F major**. Both these keys share the same key signature which contains one flat (**B♭**). The **C♯** note which occurs in this melody comes from the **D harmonic minor** scale. The piece is written in a **Baroque** style.The most famous composer from this period is **Johann Sebastian Bach**, who was a master at writing both melodically and harmonically at the same time. The harmonica did not exist in Bach's time, but one of his famous flute pieces "Siciliano" can be found on page 177.

72   **Perpetual Motion**

The accompaniment on the recording of this piece is played on a harpsichord. The whole melody is played by the harmonica and then the accompaniment repeats so you can provide the melody. This piece may take some time to master but is well worth learning.

LEARNING A NEW MINOR KEY

The process for learning a new minor key is the same as that of a major key, except that there is more than one scale involved. You will need to know the notes of the natural, harmonic and melodic minor both theoretically and on the saxophone. Written below are the notes of these three scales in the key of **D minor**. Learn them from memory and then play the following example.

C Natural minor = C D E♭ F G A♭ B♭
Formula – 1 2 ♭3 4 5 ♭6 ♭7

C Harmonic minor = C D E♭ F G A♭ B
Formula – 1 2 ♭3 4 5 ♭6 7

C Melodic minor = C D E♭ F G A B
Formula – 1 2 ♭3 4 5 6 7

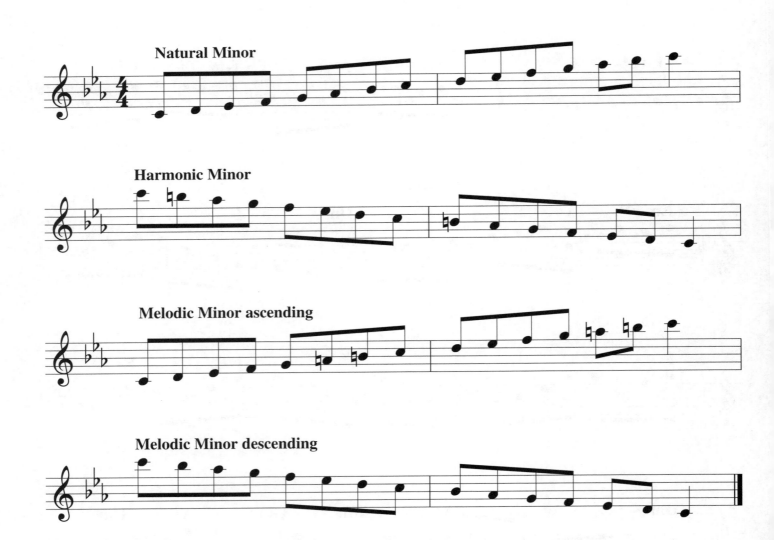

MINOR SCALES IN ALL KEYS

By simply following the formula for each type of minor scale, either by scale degrees or pattern of tones and semitones, it is possible to create any of the minor scales from any starting note. E.g. if you know that the **natural minor** scale contains **flattened 3rd, 6th and 7th degrees** and you start with the note **C**, you would come up with the following notes -

C, D, E♭, F, G, A♭, B♭, C

If you know that the **harmonic minor** scale contains **flattened 3rd, and 6th degrees**, but a **natural 7th degree**, all you have to do to change the natural minor to the harmonic minor is **sharpen the 7th degree by a semitone**. Once again if you start with the note **C**, you would come up with the following notes -

C, D, E♭, F, G, A♭, B, C

To change the harmonic minor to an **ascending melodic minor** you need to **sharpen the 6th degree by a semitone**. Starting with the note **C**, you would come up with the following notes -

C, D, E♭, F, G, A, B, C

The Classical form of the descending melodic minor is identical to the natural minor. To become familiar with the notes of minor scales in all keys, it is important to **write out the three types of minor scales starting on each of the 12 notes of the chromatic scale**.

The following examples demonstrate melodies created from the three types of minor scales.

It is also important to be able to transpose melodies in minor keys. The process is the same as for major keys - write the scale degrees under the melody notes and then work out what notes those degrees equate to in the key you want to transpose to. Shown below is an example in the key of **A minor** with the scale degrees written under the notes.

76   **A Melodic Minor**

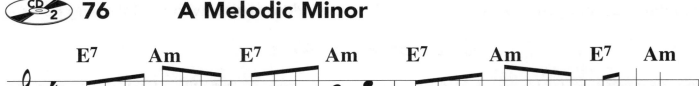

Here is the same example transposed to **F minor**. The key signature of F minor contains **four flats**, but the sixth and seventh degrees of the melodic minor are raised, so the notes **D** and **E** will be **naturals**. Remember to learn the notes of the scale first, then work out the scale degrees.

F, G, A♭, B♭, C, D♮, E♮, F

77   **F Melodic Minor**

TABLE OF MINOR SCALES

Here is a table which shows the notes of the traditional melodic minor scale in all twelve keys. Remember that the **descending melodic minor is the same as the natural minor**. To work out the notes for the **harmonic minor**, simply **flatten the 6th** degree of the ascending melodic minor.

	T	S	T	T	T	T	S	T	T	S	T	T	S	T
A MELODIC MINOR*	A	B	C	D	E	F#	G#	A	G♮	F♮	E	D	C	B	A
E MELODIC MINOR*	E	F#	G	A	B	C#	D#	E	D♮	C♮	B	A	G	F#	E
B MELODIC MINOR*	B	C#	D	E	F#	G#	A#	B	A♮	G♮	F#	E	D	C#	B
F# MELODIC MINOR*	F#	G#	A	B	C#	D#	E#	F#	E♮	D♮	C#	B	A	G#	F#
C# MELODIC MINOR*	C#	D#	E	F#	G#	A#	B#	C#	B♮	A♮	G#	F#	E	D#	C#
G# MELODIC MINOR	G#	A#	B	C#	D#	E#	G	G#	F#	E♮	D#	C#	B	A#	G#
D# MELODIC MINOR	D#	E#	F#	G#	A#	B#	D	D#	C#	B♮	A#	G#	F#	E#	D#
D MELODIC MINOR*	D	E	F	G	A	B♮	C#	D	C♮	B♭	A	G	F	E	D
G MELODIC MINOR*	G	A	B♭	C	D	E♮	F#	G	F	E♭	D	C	B♭	A	G
C MELODIC MINOR	C	D	E♭	F	G	A♮	B♮	C	B♭	A♭	G	F	E♭	D	C
F MELODIC MINOR	F	G	A♭	B♭	C	D♮	E♮	F	E♭	D♭	C	B♭	A♭	G	F
B♭ MELODIC MINOR	B♭	C	D♭	E♭	F	G♮	A♮	B	A♭	G♭	F	E♭	D♭	C	B♭
E♭ MELODIC MINOR	E♭	F	G♭	A♭	B♭	C♮	D♮	E♭	D♭	C♭	B♭	A♭	G♭	F♭	E♭
ROMAN NUMERALS	i	ii	iii	iv	v	vi	vii	viii	vii	vi	v	iv	iii	ii	i

177

To finish things off, here is a great piece by **J.S. Bach** from Sonata number 2 for flute and harpsichord. It is written in the key of **G minor** in § time. There are many great pieces written for other instruments which can also be played on the harmonica. Look for Classical flute or clarinet pieces and also Jazz saxophone solos. Keep playing, keep practicing and play with other musicians as often as possible.

78   **Siciliano**

J.S. Bach

JAM ALONG PROGRESSIONS

Congratulations on finishing the book! By now you should be sounding very good and be getting a lot of pleasure from your harmonica playing. To add to that pleasure, and help you practice everything you have learned, there are some extra tracks which have been recorded on the CD for you to jam along with. Try out any of the licks in the book with these progressions, and make a habit of improvising your own licks and solos. As well as this, you should play with other musicians as much as possible, as this will help to develop your playing and also put your licks in a musical context.

 79 Cross Harp Blues Shuffle in G

 80 Cross Harp Slow Blues in G   (With Stops)

 81 Cross Harp Country Rock in G

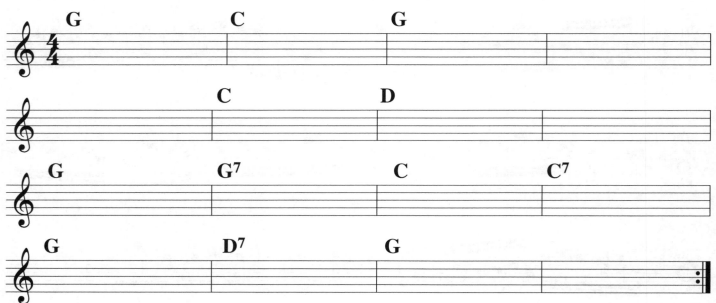

 82 3rd Position Blues in D minor

 83 4th and 1st Position Jam-Along

PERFORMING IN PUBLIC

Performing in public can be both exciting and frightening for any new performer whether they are a singer, an instrumentalist, an actor or simply someone giving a speech on a social occasion. Many people who are shy at first develop into dynamic performers who can both entertain and captivate an audience. Like any other skill, performing in public takes time to develop and there is much to be learned from watching other performers. To begin with, the best approach can be to simply take a deep breath, walk on, smile, look the audience in the eye and begin with a song you are very familiar with. If you are nervous, concentrate on the sound you and your accompanist(s) are making and move your body to the music in any way that feels good. If you are able to enjoy yourself, this will communicate itself to the audience. Nervousness can be turned into excitement and positive energy and can actually make your natural reactions and responses to the music quicker.

OVERCOMING NERVES

There are three essential elements in overcoming nervousness and turning it into a positive. The first of these is **knowing your material well**. This means thoroughly rehearsing all aspects of each song before you even consider performing them. If you are unsure of the key or which harp to use, or the notes or timing of either the melody or the accompaniment, it is not surprising that you would become nervous. The more certain you are of these things, the more you are free concentrate on expressing the meaning and feeling of each song and making great music.

The second element is **being comfortable with your equipment and your environment**. Most public performances involve the use of microphones. Using a microphone will be discussed later in this lesson. When you are on stage, it is important to be comfortable using the microphone and to not be startled by hearing yourself through the PA system or foldback speakers. If possible, it is advisable to have a sound check before members of the public arrive. Most professional ensembles have a thorough sound check in which all the equipment is tested individually and together at least an hour (preferably more) before the show. This allows everybody to become comfortable with the sound of the room as well as the equipment. If you learn a bit about PA systems you can also communicate your requirements and preferences to the person operating the sound system.

The third element is **trusting yourself**. If you are considering playing in public, you are probably fairly confident that you are making a good sound when you play and you have probably received compliments from friends as well. In this case, you should be able to play equally well or better in public, particularly once an audience begins to respond. Your body instinctively knows every aspect of producing a good sound, so it is usually just a case of "letting go" and becoming part of the music. The more you can become the character in each song (like an actor) the more convincing your performance will be and the better you will be able to deliver it.

EYE CONTACT

When you play music, you are telling a story to the audience. Look at them as you tell this story and they will respond. Obviously you cannot look at everybody, but you can pick out certain people (e.g. someone wearing bright clothing or someone with a bald spot on their head). Another option is to look towards the people in the middle of the audience. Change your focus from time to time to include all sections of the audience. Everybody will feel you are communicating with them personally and will enjoy your performance more. Remember that when people go to hear a public performance, they are looking forward to having a good time. This means they are automatically prepared to like you even before they see or hear you, so in reality the performance should be a positive experience for everyone involved. Another important aspect of any performance is eye contact between the performers. The fact that an ensemble are communicating well and obviously enjoying themselves makes the audience feel good too.

STAGE PRESENCE AND STAGE CRAFT

Most great performers have what is commonly known as good **stage presence**. Stage presence is the total impression created in the minds and emotions of the audience by the performer(s). This impression is made up of both the drama of the music and speech and the drama of the visual performance. As mentioned earlier, there is much to be learned by watching other performers. It is essential for aspiring performers to see professional musicians, singers, actors or other entertainers perform live as often as possible in the early stages. You can do this by going to shows or by watching performances on video or television. Notice how each performer communicates with both their ensemble and the audience. Learn how they use both spontaneous and choreographed movement. Watch how the music is expressed through their bodies and facial expressions as well as their sound. Notice whether they use humour or not, or any other element of public performance you can think of. All these things can be learned and developed and can be described as the various parts of stage craft.

DEVELOPING YOUR OWN STYLE

Many performers learn their stage craft and their ability to express their vocal or instrumental technique by copying other performers at first and then ultimately adapting what they have learned to form their own unique style and presence. Junior Wells seriously studied Little Walter's style of singing and playing early in his career, but later developed his own intensely personal style which has little in common with Little Walter. This is similar to the way students of visual art are taught to copy the works of masters early in their development. By doing this, the student learns about color, form, design, balance, etc. as well as learning technique. However, this is only the first step in the process. The idea is to master the practical elements in order to be able to go on and express your own feelings, ideas and personality through your own work. Copying a Rembrandt or Picasso painting is an extremely valuable exercise for an art student, but it is not an end in itself. So it is with playing and performing. Learn all you can from performers you admire, whether it is their technique, their musicianship or their stagecraft. Study them in detail and work diligently on everything you learn, particularly in the early stages of your development. However, it is not recommended that you slavishly copy any particular person's style over a long period of time (unless you want to be a comedy act). As your confidence develops along with your personal feelings for the music you are performing, your own style will begin to emerge by itself if you let it. As you practice and perform, notice the things that you feel most intensely about. These are the seeds which will grow into your own vital style if you are true to them and develop them properly.

MICROPHONES

It is essential for all harmonica players to know how to use a microphone. Even if you mainly in small rooms with only a guitar accompaniment, it is likely that you will be required to use a microphone at some stage. If you play with a band, you will use a microphone every time you perform. It is a good idea to have your own microphone that you are comfortable with, even if the venue you are performing at provides them along with the PA system.

MICROPHONES FOR PERFORMING LIVE

There are several different types of microphones available. Each of them is best suited to a different musical situation (e.g. live band performance, or recording session).
The type of microphone most commonly used for live performances is the **dynamic microphone**. These microphones contain a diaphragm and a coil which is activated when the voice causes it to vibrate. Dynamic microphones are normally uni-directional, or "front sensitive" which means that sounds entering from the sides of the microphone are amplified less than sound entering from the top or front. Because of their resistance to feedback (the piercing sound made when a microphone picks up the sound coming from the speakers and amplifies it again) uni-directional microphones are particularly useful in a live band environment.

Microphones which are omni-directional receive sound equally from all sides of the microphone. This makes them useful for back-up vocals in situations where two or more singers share one microphone but they are not recommended for a lead singer in a live band situation.

Before you buy a microphone it is advisable to visit a music store and try out some in the store. The Shure SM58 microphone shown in the photo below is a typical professional quality uni-directional dynamic microphone and is one of the most common microphones used by bands when a clean, natural sound is required. There are also other good microphones available which are of a similar design. If you intend to perform in public regularly, it is worth spending a little extra on a good microphone as it will make you sound better and make you more comfortable with your sound on stage.

Shure SM58 - A Typical Dynamic Microphone

AMPLIFICATION

When playing with a band, it is often necessary to amplify your harmonica. This can be done by using a harmonica microphone such as a Shure "green bullet" (shown below) and plugging it into an amplifier (usually a guitar amplifier) or by playing directly into a vocal microphone through a PA system. It takes practice to play well with amplification, so if possible it is best to rehearse regularly with your amplified sound before playing live.

Although you can easily play with a vocal mic on a stand, it is more common to hold a harp mic in your left hand and control the harp with your right hand when playing amplified. This takes practice and is worth developing at home and in rehearsal before attempting it on stage. You may experience problems with unwanted "feedback" at first. This can be overcome by not standing too close the front of the amp and adjusting the volume and tone knobs on the am until you get a good strong but controlled sound.

"Green Bullet" Harmonica Microphone

Electric Triode Valve Amplifier

OVERDRIVE

One of the advantages of using a harp mic such as a green bullet and running it through an amp is that this enables you to get a distorted or "overdriven" sound which sustains more and sounds more electric than a harp played through a vocal mic. Listen to players like Little Walter, Big Walter Horton (another master of Chicago Blues) and Rod Piazza to hear great examples of amplified harp playing. There are no rights or wrongs with amplified playing. It is simply a matter of personal taste.

USING A HARMONICA RACK

As mentioned earlier in the book, it is a good idea to learn a bit about guitar or keyboard playing in order to improve your all round knowledge of music. Being able to play one of these instruments means you can also accompany yourself when you play harmonica. There is a device called a **harmonica rack** which holds the harmonica and fits over your head - resting on your shoulders, thus leaving your hands free to play guitar or keyboards. Many singer-songwriters (e.g. Bob Dylan and Neil Young) have used harmonica racks to give them more options as a solo performer.

Most music stores which sell instruments carry harmonic racks or can at least order them. It takes time to learn to play two instruments at one, but like everything else, it is simply a matter of practice. Start with simple melodies and rhythm parts until you develop some basic co-ordination and you are on your way.

LISTENING

Apart from books, your most important source of information as a musician will be recordings. Listen to albums which feature harp players. Some important Blues players to look out for are: Sonny Terry, Little Walter, Sonny Boy Williamson, Junior Wells, Big Walter Horton, James Cotton, Billy Branch, Paul Butterfield, Snooky Pryor, Jerry Portnoy, Sugar Blue, Charlie Musselwhite and Rod Piazza.

For Country , Folk and Rock playing, listen to Charlie McCoy, Brendan Power, as well as the simple but effective playing of Neil Young and Bob Dylan. Some of the best **Chromatic** harmonica players include Larry Adler, Toots Thielemans and Stevie Wonder.

There are also numerous great Jazz and Blues sax players who are worth checking out. Little Walter got a lot of his ideas from listening to sax players. Some of the most Bluesy sax players are: Maceo Parker and Pee Wee Ellis (Solo or with James Brown) King Curtis, Junior Walker, Fathead Newman, A.C. Reed, Eddie Shaw, Eddie "Cleanhead" Vinson, Scott Page, Illinois Jacquet, Stanley Turrentine, Eddie Harris, Ben Webster, Johnny Hodges, and Roland Kirk who often played two saxophones at a time!

Guitar Players are another good source of ideas. Listen to the guitarist on any Blues album and you will hear note bending, slides, grace notes and other techniques which are equally effective on the harmonica. Some guitarists to look out for are BB King, Otis Rush, Buddy Guy (with Junior Wells or solo), Magic Sam, Lightnin' Hopkins and Albert Collins along with Robert Junior Lockwood and Luther Tucker who can both be found on albums by Sonny Boy Williamson.

When you are listening to albums, try to sing along with the solos and visualize which holes you would play and the techniques you would use to achieve the sounds you are hearing. This helps you absorb the music and before long, it starts to come out in your own playing. It is also valuable to play along with albums, sometimes imitating what you are hearing and other times improvising. This is very good ear training and is also a lot of fun.

TRANSCRIBING

As well as playing along with albums and imitating what you hear, it is important to work out solos and melodies you admire exactly and write them down. This is called **transcribing**. By doing this, you can analyse the player's note choices and rhythmic idiosyncrasies and find out exactly what makes them sound the way they do. By doing this, you will be able to analyze the lines to understand what it is you like about them and then incorporate them into your own playing. It is important to transcribe a variety of players from different eras rather than just imitating one favorite (who wants to be a clone?). You will learn something different from each player and will also open yourself up to new ideas and new sounds.

All the great players have done lots of transcribing. Make it part of your daily practice routine. When you have memorized a new melody or solo, try playing it with a play along recording of the song it came from or one with a similar progression (e.g. a Blues). Once you can play the solo perfectly, use it as a basis for improvising and then use the ideas you come up with next time you play with other musicians. Make a habit of this and your playing will never stop developing.

RECORDING YOURSELF

From time to time it is a good idea to record your performances or practice sessions. Unless you have studio quality equipment, the tone quality you hear on the recording may not be completely accurate, but any recording will pick up timing and relative pitch accurately. As you listen back to yourself, pay particular attention to areas you think are particularly weak or particularly strong. Anything you think sounds good is worth developing further and anything that doesn't (e.g. timing, or pitching on bent notes) should be the focus of your practice sessions until it is turned into a strength.

LEARNING MORE ABOUT MUSIC

Regardless of your aspirations, your playing will benefit from learning as much about music as you can. By now you should have a good basic understanding of how melody and rhythm works, how beats can be subdivided and what keys are. However, many harmonica players don't know much about chords or harmony (e.g. keyboard or rhythm guitar accompaniment). If you have a basic understanding of these subjects you can contribute much more to band arrangements and songwriting. In fact, it is strongly recommended that you learn at least a bit of general music by taking up bass, guitar or keyboards. Ask the other musicians you play with about what they are doing and get them to show you a few things. Of course, the harmonica will still be your main instrument, but harp players who understand music are always popular and usually get lots of work.

For more books and recordings by Peter Gelling, visit: **www.bentnotes.com**